Healthy

High protein

Lunch Ideas

Easy, simple & delicious recipe cookbook to energize your noon with delicious and nutritious meals

MATTHEW REYNOLDS

Disclaimer

The information provided in this book is for general informational purposes only. While every effort has been made to provide accurate and up-to-date information, the author and publisher make no representations or warranties of any kind, express or implied, about the completeness, accuracy, reliability, suitability, or availability of the information contained within this book. Any reliance you place on such information is strictly at your own risk.

Allergies: The recipes included in this book may contain a wide variety of ingredients, and some of them may be common allergens, such as nuts, soy, wheat, or others. It is crucial for readers to be aware of their own allergies and the allergies of those for whom they are preparing food. While efforts have been made to identify potential allergens in the recipes, the author and publisher cannot guarantee that allergenic ingredients are not present in trace amounts due to cross-contamination or other factors.

The author and publisher strongly recommend that readers with known food allergies exercise caution and consult with a qualified healthcare professional or allergist before preparing and consuming any recipe from this book. It is the responsibility of the reader to verify the ingredients used and to make informed decisions regarding their dietary choices.

The author and publisher shall not be held liable for any loss, damage, or injury resulting from the use or misuse of the information presented in this book, including allergic reactions. The author and publisher do not endorse any specific products, brands, or services mentioned in this book.

Medical Advice: The recipes and nutritional information provided in this book are intended for educational and illustrative purposes only. They are not meant to substitute for professional dietary, nutritional, or medical advice. Readers are encouraged to consult with a qualified healthcare or nutrition professional before making dietary or lifestyle changes, especially if they have specific dietary restrictions, allergies, or medical conditions

Loved the book? Don't forget to leave a review.

Table of Contents

Grilled Chicken Quinoa Bowl

Ingredients:

- 1 pound boneless, skinless chicken breasts

- 1 cup quinoa

- 2 cups low-sodium chicken broth

- 2 tablespoons olive oil

- 1 teaspoon paprika

- 1 teaspoon garlic powder

- Salt and pepper, to taste

- 2 cups mixed vegetables (e.g., bell peppers, broccoli, carrots)

- 1 cup cherry tomatoes, halved

- 1/2 cup cucumber, diced

- 1/4 cup red onion, finely chopped

- 1/4 cup fresh parsley, chopped

- Juice of 1 lemon

Instructions:

1. **Prepare the Quinoa:**

   - Rinse quinoa under cold water until the water runs clear.

   - In a medium saucepan, bring the chicken broth to a boil.

   - Add quinoa, reduce heat to low, cover, and simmer for about 15-20 minutes, or until all liquid is absorbed and quinoa is tender.

   - Remove from heat, fluff with a fork, and let it cool.

2. **Marinate the Chicken:**

   - In a bowl, combine olive oil, paprika, garlic powder, salt, and pepper to create a marinade.

   - Place chicken breasts in a resealable bag or shallow dish and pour the marinade over them.

   - Seal the bag or cover the dish and refrigerate for at least 30 minutes, or overnight for best results.

3. **Grill the Chicken:**

- Preheat your grill to medium-high heat.

- Remove chicken from the marinade and grill for about 6-8 minutes per side or until the internal temperature reaches 165°F (74°C) and the chicken is no longer pink in the center.

- Let the chicken rest for a few minutes before slicing it into thin strips.

4. **Prepare the Vegetables:**

- While the chicken is grilling, brush the mixed vegetables with a little olive oil and season with salt and pepper.

- Grill the vegetables until they are tender and slightly charred, about 5-7 minutes.

5. **Assemble the Bowl:**

- In a large bowl, combine the cooked quinoa, grilled chicken, grilled vegetables, cherry tomatoes, cucumber, red onion, and fresh parsley.

- Squeeze the lemon juice over the bowl and gently toss everything together to combine.

Nutritional Information (Per Serving):

- Calories: 400

- Protein: 30g

- Carbohydrates: 35g

- Fiber: 6g

- Sugars: 4g

- Fat: 15g

- Saturated Fat: 2g

- Cholesterol: 65mg

- Sodium: 350mg

- Vitamin C: 50% DV

- Vitamin A: 20% DV

- Iron: 15% DV

Summary:

This Grilled Chicken Quinoa Bowl is a delicious and nutritious high-protein meal. Grilled chicken, flavorful quinoa, and a medley of grilled vegetables come together to create a balanced and satisfying dish.

Packed with protein, fiber, vitamins, and minerals, it's perfect for a healthy lunch or dinner option.

Tips and Tricks:

- You can use chicken thighs or tofu as a chicken substitute for different flavors.

- Customize your bowl with your favorite veggies, herbs, or a drizzle of your preferred dressing.

- Make extra quinoa to have on hand for quick and easy meal prep during the week.

- Grill the vegetables ahead of time to save even more time on busy days.

Ingredient Substitutions:

- Use vegetable broth or water instead of chicken broth for cooking quinoa to make it vegetarian.

- Feel free to swap quinoa with brown rice or cauliflower rice for a different grain base.

- Experiment with different marinades or seasonings for the chicken to vary the flavors.

Salmon and Asparagus Salad

Ingredients:

- 2 salmon fillets

- 1 bunch asparagus spears

- 2 cups mixed greens

- 1/4 cup cherry tomatoes, halved

- 2 tablespoons olive oil

- 1 tablespoon balsamic vinegar

- Salt and pepper, to taste

- Lemon wedges for garnish

Instructions:

1. **Prepare the Salmon and Asparagus:**

   - Preheat your oven to 400°F (200°C).

   - Place salmon fillets and asparagus on a baking sheet.

   - Drizzle with olive oil, season with salt and pepper, and bake for about 12-15 minutes until the salmon flakes easily and the asparagus is tender.

2. **Assemble the Salad:**

   - In a large bowl, arrange mixed greens and cherry tomatoes.

   - Top with the cooked salmon and asparagus.

3. **Make the Dressing:**

   - In a small bowl, whisk together olive oil and balsamic vinegar.

   - Drizzle the dressing over the salad.

4. **Garnish and Serve:**

   - Garnish with lemon wedges and serve immediately.

Nutritional Information (Per Serving):

- Calories: 350

- Protein: 30g

- Carbohydrates: 10g

- Fiber: 3g

- Sugars: 3g

- Fat: 20g

- Saturated Fat: 3g

- Cholesterol: 75mg

- Sodium: 80mg

- Vitamin C: 15% DV

- Vitamin A: 40% DV

- Iron: 20% DV

Summary:

This Salmon and Asparagus Salad is a light yet protein-packed meal featuring tender salmon, roasted asparagus, and a bed of fresh greens. The balsamic dressing adds a delightful tanginess to this nutritious salad.

Tips and Tricks:

- Try grilling the salmon and asparagus for a different flavor profile.

- Customize the salad with your favorite greens and additional veggies.

Ingredient Substitutions:

- Replace salmon with grilled chicken or tofu if desired.

Black Bean and Avocado Wrap

Ingredients:

- 1 (15-ounce) can black beans, drained and rinsed
- 1 ripe avocado, mashed
- 1/2 cup diced red bell pepper
- 1/4 cup diced red onion
- 1/4 cup chopped fresh cilantro
- 1 teaspoon ground cumin
- Salt and pepper, to taste
- 4 whole wheat tortillas

Instructions:

1. **Prepare the Filling:**

   - In a bowl, combine black beans, mashed avocado, red bell pepper, red onion, cilantro, cumin, salt, and pepper. Mix well.

2. **Assemble the Wraps:**

   - Lay out the whole wheat tortillas.

- Divide the black bean and avocado mixture evenly among the tortillas.

3. **Wrap and Serve:**

    - Fold in the sides of each tortilla, then roll them up from the bottom to create wraps.

Nutritional Information (Per Serving):

- Calories: 320

- Protein: 10g

- Carbohydrates: 50g

- Fiber: 12g

- Sugars: 4g

- Fat: 12g

- Saturated Fat: 2g

- Cholesterol: 0mg

- Sodium: 400mg

- Vitamin C: 60% DV

- Vitamin A: 10% DV

- Iron: 15% DV

Summary:

This Black Bean and Avocado Wrap is a quick and easy lunch option packed with plant-based protein and fiber. The combination of black beans and creamy avocado, along with the crunch of red bell pepper and cilantro, makes for a flavorful and satisfying wrap.

Tips and Tricks:

- Add a dash of hot sauce or a sprinkle of cheese for extra flavor.

- Customize with your favorite veggies or a squeeze of lime juice.

Ingredient Substitutions:

- Use spinach or whole grain lettuce leaves instead of tortillas for a low-carb option.

Greek Yogurt Tuna Salad

Ingredients:

- 2 (5-ounce) cans of tuna in water, drained
- 1/2 cup Greek yogurt
- 1/4 cup diced red onion
- 1/4 cup diced cucumber
- 1/4 cup diced celery
- 1 tablespoon fresh dill, chopped
- Juice of 1 lemon
- Salt and pepper, to taste
- Whole grain crackers or lettuce leaves for serving

Instructions:

1. **Prepare the Tuna Salad:**

   - In a bowl, combine drained tuna, Greek yogurt, red onion, cucumber, celery, dill, lemon juice, salt, and pepper. Mix well.

2. **Serve the Salad:**

- Serve the Greek Yogurt Tuna Salad on whole grain crackers or lettuce leaves.

Nutritional Information (Per Serving, Salad Only):

- Calories: 250

- Protein: 30g

- Carbohydrates: 8g

- Fiber: 1g

- Sugars: 4g

- Fat: 10g

- Saturated Fat: 2g

- Cholesterol: 55mg

- Sodium: 400mg

- Vitamin C: 10% DV

- Vitamin A: 2% DV

- Iron: 15% DV

Summary:

This Greek Yogurt Tuna Salad is a protein-packed twist on a classic tuna salad. Greek yogurt adds creaminess and extra protein while keeping it light and healthy. Enjoy it on whole grain crackers or lettuce leaves for a satisfying meal.

Tips and Tricks:

- Add chopped olives or cherry tomatoes for extra flavor.

- Serve on whole wheat bread as a sandwich if preferred.

Ingredient Substitutions:

- Substitute Greek yogurt with mayonnaise or mashed avocado if desired.

Spinach and Feta Stuffed Chicken

Ingredients:

- 4 boneless, skinless chicken breasts
- 2 cups fresh spinach leaves
- 1/2 cup crumbled feta cheese
- 1/4 cup sun-dried tomatoes, chopped
- 1 clove garlic, minced
- 1 tablespoon olive oil
- Salt and pepper, to taste
- Toothpicks or kitchen twine

Instructions:

1. **Prepare the Filling:**

   - In a skillet, heat olive oil over medium heat.
   - Add minced garlic and sauté for about 1 minute until fragrant.
   - Add fresh spinach leaves and cook until wilted.

- Remove from heat and stir in crumbled feta cheese and chopped sun-dried tomatoes.

2. **Stuffed the Chicken:**

    - Preheat your oven to 375°F (190°C).

    - Make a horizontal slit in each chicken breast to create a pocket.

    - Stuff each chicken breast with the spinach, feta, and tomato mixture.

    - Secure with toothpicks or kitchen twine.

3. **Cook the Chicken:**

    - Season the stuffed chicken breasts with salt and pepper.

    - Heat a skillet over medium-high heat and sear each chicken breast for about 2-3 minutes per side until golden brown.

    - Transfer the chicken to a baking dish and bake in the preheated oven for about 20-25 minutes, or until the chicken is cooked through.

4. **Serve:**

- Remove the toothpicks or twine before serving.

Nutritional Information (Per Serving):

- Calories: 280

- Protein: 40g

- Carbohydrates: 5g

- Fiber: 2g

- Sugars: 2g

- Fat: 10g

- Saturated Fat: 4g

- Cholesterol: 110mg

- Sodium: 450mg

- Vitamin C: 15% DV

- Vitamin A: 35% DV

- Iron: 10% DV

Summary:

This Spinach and Feta Stuffed Chicken is a flavorful and protein-rich dish that combines tender chicken breasts with a delicious spinach, feta, and sun-dried tomato filling. It's an impressive yet easy-to-make meal for any occasion.

Tips and Tricks:

- Use toothpicks or kitchen twine to secure the filling inside the chicken breasts.

- Experiment with different cheese varieties or add herbs for extra flavor.

Ingredient Substitutions:

- Swap feta cheese with goat cheese or mozzarella for a different taste.

Lentil and Chickpea Curry

Ingredients:

- 1 cup dried green or brown lentils, rinsed and drained
- 1 (15-ounce) can chickpeas, drained and rinsed
- 1 onion, finely chopped
- 2 cloves garlic, minced
- 1 tablespoon olive oil
- 2 tablespoons curry powder
- 1 teaspoon ground cumin
- 1/2 teaspoon ground coriander
- 1/2 teaspoon ground turmeric
- 1/4 teaspoon cayenne pepper (adjust to taste)
- 1 (14-ounce) can diced tomatoes
- 1 (14-ounce) can coconut milk
- Salt and pepper, to taste
- Fresh cilantro, for garnish

- Cooked brown rice or whole wheat naan, for serving

Instructions:

1. **Cook the Lentils:**

   - In a large pot, heat olive oil over medium heat.

   - Add chopped onion and garlic, and sauté until softened, about 3-5 minutes.

   - Stir in curry powder, cumin, coriander, turmeric, and cayenne pepper. Cook for another minute until fragrant.

   - Add diced tomatoes, lentils, and chickpeas to the pot.

   - Pour in the coconut milk and stir to combine.

   - Season with salt and pepper.

   - Bring to a simmer, cover, and let it cook for about 20-25 minutes, or until the lentils are tender and the sauce has thickened.

2. **Serve:**

- Serve the lentil and chickpea curry over cooked brown rice or with whole wheat naan.

- Garnish with fresh cilantro.

Nutritional Information (Per Serving, Curry Only):

- Calories: 300

- Protein: 14g

- Carbohydrates: 35g

- Fiber: 11g

- Sugars: 7g

- Fat: 14g

- Saturated Fat: 9g

- Cholesterol: 0mg

- Sodium: 350mg

- Vitamin C: 25% DV

- Vitamin A: 10% DV

- Iron: 25% DV

Summary:

This Lentil and Chickpea Curry is a hearty and protein-rich vegetarian dish with a flavorful blend of spices. It's packed with plant-based protein, fiber, and essential nutrients. Serve it with brown rice or whole wheat naan for a complete and satisfying meal.

Tips and Tricks:

- Adjust the level of spiciness by varying the amount of cayenne pepper.

- Customize with your favorite vegetables, such as spinach or bell peppers.

Ingredient Substitutions:

- Use red lentils instead of green or brown lentils for a quicker cooking time.

Turkey and Veggie Stir-Fry

Ingredients:

- 1 pound ground turkey
- 2 cups mixed vegetables (e.g., bell peppers, broccoli, carrots)
- 2 cloves garlic, minced
- 1 tablespoon ginger, minced
- 2 tablespoons low-sodium soy sauce
- 1 tablespoon hoisin sauce
- 1 teaspoon sesame oil
- 1 tablespoon olive oil
- Cooked brown rice or cauliflower rice, for serving
- Green onions, for garnish

Instructions:

1. **Cook the Ground Turkey:**

   - In a large skillet or wok, heat olive oil over medium-high heat.

- Add minced garlic and ginger, and sauté for about 1 minute until fragrant.

- Add ground turkey and cook until browned and cooked through, breaking it into crumbles as it cooks.

2. **Stir-Fry the Vegetables:**

- Add mixed vegetables to the skillet and stir-fry for about 5-7 minutes until they are tender-crisp.

3. **Make the Sauce:**

- In a small bowl, whisk together low-sodium soy sauce, hoisin sauce, and sesame oil.

4. **Combine and Serve:**

- Pour the sauce over the turkey and vegetables in the skillet.

- Stir to coat everything evenly with the sauce.

- Serve the turkey and vegetable stir-fry over cooked brown rice or cauliflower rice.

- Garnish with sliced green onions.

Nutritional Information (Per Serving, Stir-Fry Only):

- Calories: 350

- Protein: 30g

- Carbohydrates: 15g

- Fiber: 4g

- Sugars: 4g

- Fat: 18g

- Saturated Fat: 4g

- Cholesterol: 80mg

- Sodium: 600mg

- Vitamin C: 60% DV

- Vitamin A: 40% DV

- Iron: 15% DV

Summary:

This Turkey and Veggie Stir-Fry is a quick and flavorful high-protein meal. Ground turkey and a colorful mix of vegetables are stir-fried together and coated in a savory sauce. Serve it over brown rice or cauliflower rice for a satisfying dinner.

Tips and Tricks:

- Customize the vegetables to your liking and what's in season.

- Add a touch of sriracha for extra heat, if desired.

Ingredient Substitutions:

- Substitute ground chicken or tofu for the ground turkey.

Quinoa and Chickpea Power Bowl

Ingredients:

- 1 cup quinoa, rinsed and drained
- 2 cups low-sodium vegetable broth
- 1 (15-ounce) can chickpeas, drained and rinsed
- 2 cups mixed greens
- 1 cup cherry tomatoes, halved
- 1/2 cucumber, diced
- 1/4 cup red onion, finely chopped
- 1/4 cup fresh parsley, chopped
- Juice of 1 lemon
- 2 tablespoons olive oil
- Salt and pepper, to taste

Instructions:

1. **Prepare the Quinoa:**

   - In a medium saucepan, bring the vegetable broth to a boil.

- Add quinoa, reduce heat to low, cover, and simmer for about 15-20 minutes, or until all liquid is absorbed and quinoa is tender.

- Remove from heat, fluff with a fork, and let it cool.

2. **Assemble the Bowl:**

   - In a large bowl, combine the cooked quinoa, chickpeas, mixed greens, cherry tomatoes, cucumber, red onion, and fresh parsley.

3. **Make the Dressing:**

   - In a small bowl, whisk together lemon juice, olive oil, salt, and pepper.

4. **Drizzle and Toss:**

   - Drizzle the dressing over the bowl and gently toss everything together to combine.

Nutritional Information (Per Serving):

- Calories: 380

- Protein: 12g

- Carbohydrates: 56g

- Fiber: 10g

- Sugars: 5g

- Fat: 15g

- Saturated Fat: 2g

- Cholesterol: 0mg

- Sodium: 350mg

- Vitamin C: 40% DV

- Vitamin A: 25% DV

- Iron: 25% DV

Summary:

This Quinoa and Chickpea Power Bowl is a nutrient-packed, high-protein meal that's both satisfying and flavorful. With quinoa, chickpeas, and a variety of fresh veggies, it's an excellent choice for a nutritious lunch or dinner.

Tips and Tricks:

- Customize the bowl with your favorite veggies or add avocado for creaminess.

- Make extra quinoa and store it in the fridge for quick and easy meal prep.

Ingredient Substitutions:

- Use vegetable or chicken broth instead of vegetable broth for cooking quinoa if preferred.

Shrimp and Broccoli Quiche

Ingredients:

- 1 pre-made whole wheat pie crust
- 1 cup cooked shrimp, peeled and deveined
- 1 cup broccoli florets, blanched and chopped
- 1/2 cup low-fat shredded cheddar cheese
- 4 large eggs
- 1 cup low-fat milk
- 1/4 teaspoon salt
- 1/4 teaspoon black pepper
- 1/4 teaspoon paprika
- 1/4 teaspoon dried thyme

Instructions:

1. **Preheat the Oven:**
   - Preheat your oven to 375°F (190°C).
2. **Prepare the Crust:**

- Place the whole wheat pie crust in a pie dish and set aside.

3. **Layer the Fillings:**

   - Evenly distribute the cooked shrimp, blanched broccoli, and shredded cheddar cheese over the pie crust.

4. **Prepare the Egg Mixture:**

   - In a bowl, whisk together eggs, milk, salt, black pepper, paprika, and dried thyme until well combined.

5. **Pour and Bake:**

   - Pour the egg mixture over the shrimp, broccoli, and cheese in the pie crust.

6. **Bake:**

   - Place the quiche in the preheated oven and bake for 35-40 minutes or until the center is set and the top is golden brown.

7. **Cool and Serve:**

   - Allow the quiche to cool slightly before slicing and serving.

Nutritional Information (Per Serving, 1/8 of Quiche):

- Calories: 220

- Protein: 16g

- Carbohydrates: 15g

- Fiber: 2g

- Sugars: 2g

- Fat: 10g

- Saturated Fat: 4g

- Cholesterol: 160mg

- Sodium: 330mg

- Vitamin C: 25% DV

- Vitamin A: 15% DV

- Iron: 15% DV

Summary:

This Shrimp and Broccoli Quiche is a protein-rich and flavorful dish that's perfect for a hearty brunch or lunch. Packed with shrimp, broccoli, and cheese, it's a satisfying and nutritious meal.

Tips and Tricks:

- Customize the quiche with your favorite vegetables or herbs.

- Make it ahead of time and reheat for quick meals during the week.

Ingredient Substitutions:

- Use cooked chicken or tofu as a substitute for shrimp.

Tofu and Veggie Skewers

Ingredients:

- 1 block extra-firm tofu, pressed and cubed
- 2 cups mixed vegetables (e.g., bell peppers, zucchini, mushrooms)
- 2 tablespoons olive oil
- 2 tablespoons low-sodium soy sauce
- 1 tablespoon maple syrup or honey
- 1 teaspoon minced garlic
- 1/2 teaspoon ground ginger
- Wooden skewers, soaked in water

Instructions:

1. **Prepare the Tofu and Vegetables:**

   - Cut the pressed tofu into cubes and set aside.
   - Cut the mixed vegetables into bite-sized pieces.

2. **Make the Marinade:**

- In a bowl, whisk together olive oil, soy sauce, maple syrup (or honey), minced garlic, and ground ginger.

3. **Marinate the Tofu and Vegetables:**

   - Place the tofu and mixed vegetables in a shallow dish or resealable bag.

   - Pour the marinade over the tofu and vegetables.

   - Gently toss to coat and let it marinate for at least 30 minutes, or longer if time allows.

4. **Assemble the Skewers:**

   - Preheat your grill to medium-high heat.

   - Thread the marinated tofu and vegetables onto the soaked wooden skewers, alternating between tofu and veggies.

5. **Grill the Skewers:**

   - Grill the tofu and vegetable skewers for about 10-12 minutes, turning occasionally until they are slightly charred and heated through.

6. **Serve:**

  - Remove from the grill and serve hot.

Nutritional Information (Per Serving, 2 Skewers):

- Calories: 220

- Protein: 12g

- Carbohydrates: 18g

- Fiber: 3g

- Sugars: 8g

- Fat: 12g

- Saturated Fat: 2g

- Cholesterol: 0mg

- Sodium: 380mg

- Vitamin C: 45% DV

- Vitamin A: 20% DV

- Iron: 15% DV

Summary:

These Tofu and Veggie Skewers are a delicious and protein-packed option for a healthy lunch or dinner. Marinated tofu and a variety of colorful vegetables make for a satisfying and flavorful meal straight from the grill.

Tips and Tricks:

- Customize the skewers with your favorite vegetables and herbs.

- Use metal skewers if you don't have wooden ones.

Ingredient Substitutions:

- Swap tofu with tempeh or your preferred protein source.

Bison and Sweet Potato Hash

Ingredients:

- 1 pound ground bison
- 2 sweet potatoes, peeled and diced
- 1 red bell pepper, diced
- 1 onion, diced
- 2 cloves garlic, minced
- 1 teaspoon smoked paprika
- 1/2 teaspoon cumin
- Salt and pepper, to taste
- 2 tablespoons olive oil
- Fresh cilantro, for garnish
- Fried or poached eggs (optional)

Instructions:

1. **Cook the Sweet Potatoes:**
   - In a large skillet, heat olive oil over medium-high heat.

- Add diced sweet potatoes and cook for about 10-12 minutes, or until they are tender and slightly crispy.

- Remove the sweet potatoes from the skillet and set them aside.

2. **Cook the Bison and Veggies:**

   - In the same skillet, add ground bison and cook until browned, breaking it into crumbles as it cooks.

   - Add diced red bell pepper, onion, and minced garlic. Cook until the vegetables are softened.

3. **Combine and Season:**

   - Return the cooked sweet potatoes to the skillet with the bison and vegetables.

   - Stir in smoked paprika, cumin, salt, and pepper. Cook for an additional 2-3 minutes to blend flavors.

4. **Serve:**

   - Garnish with fresh cilantro and top with fried or poached eggs if desired.

Nutritional Information (Per Serving):

- Calories: 350
- Protein: 22g
- Carbohydrates: 26g
- Fiber: 4g
- Sugars: 7g
- Fat: 18g
- Saturated Fat: 5g
- Cholesterol: 60mg
- Sodium: 85mg
- Vitamin C: 50% DV
- Vitamin A: 240% DV
- Iron: 15% DV

Summary:

This Bison and Sweet Potato Hash is a hearty and protein-packed dish that combines ground bison, sweet potatoes, and colorful veggies with smoky spices. It's a flavorful option for a nutritious breakfast or brunch.

Tips and Tricks:

- Adjust the level of spiciness by adding chili powder or red pepper flakes.

- Customize with your favorite herbs or cheese.

Ingredient Substitutions:

- Substitute ground beef or turkey for bison if preferred.

Greek Turkey Meatballs

Ingredients:

- 1 pound ground turkey
- 1/2 cup breadcrumbs (whole wheat or gluten-free)
- 1/4 cup grated Parmesan cheese
- 1/4 cup chopped fresh parsley
- 1/4 cup diced red onion
- 1 clove garlic, minced
- 1 teaspoon dried oregano
- 1/2 teaspoon dried basil
- Salt and pepper, to taste
- Olive oil, for cooking
- Tzatziki sauce, for serving
- Lemon wedges, for garnish

Instructions:

1. **Prepare the Meatball Mixture:**

- In a large bowl, combine ground turkey, breadcrumbs, grated Parmesan cheese, chopped parsley, diced red onion, minced garlic, dried oregano, dried basil, salt, and pepper.

- Mix until all ingredients are well combined.

2. **Form Meatballs:**

- Shape the mixture into meatballs, about 1-2 inches in diameter.

3. **Cook the Meatballs:**

- Heat olive oil in a skillet over medium-high heat.

- Add the meatballs and cook for about 6-8 minutes, turning frequently, until they are browned on all sides and cooked through.

4. **Serve:**

- Serve the Greek Turkey Meatballs with tzatziki sauce for dipping.

- Garnish with lemon wedges.

Nutritional Information (Per Serving, 4 Meatballs):

- Calories: 280

- Protein: 28g

- Carbohydrates: 10g

- Fiber: 1g

- Sugars: 1g

- Fat: 14g

- Saturated Fat: 4g

- Cholesterol: 85mg

- Sodium: 400mg

- Vitamin C: 10% DV

- Vitamin A: 6% DV

- Iron: 10% DV

Summary:

These Greek Turkey Meatballs are a flavorful and protein-rich option for a tasty meal. Made with ground turkey and Mediterranean-inspired spices, they're perfect for serving as an appetizer or main course.

Tips and Tricks:

- Serve with pita bread or as a sandwich with fresh veggies and tzatziki sauce.

- Double the recipe for meal prep and freeze for later.

Ingredient Substitutions:

- Use ground chicken or beef if you prefer a different protein.

Edamame and Brown Rice Salad

Ingredients:

- 2 cups cooked brown rice, cooled
- 1 cup shelled edamame, cooked and cooled
- 1 red bell pepper, diced
- 1 carrot, grated
- 1/4 cup sliced green onions
- 1/4 cup chopped fresh cilantro
- 1/4 cup chopped fresh mint
- 1/4 cup toasted sesame seeds
- Juice of 1 lime
- 2 tablespoons low-sodium soy sauce
- 1 tablespoon rice vinegar
- 1 tablespoon honey or agave nectar
- 1 teaspoon grated fresh ginger
- 1 clove garlic, minced
- Salt and pepper, to taste

Instructions:

1. **Prepare the Dressing:**

   - In a small bowl, whisk together lime juice, soy sauce, rice vinegar, honey or agave nectar, grated ginger, minced garlic, salt, and pepper. Set aside.

2. **Combine Ingredients:**

   - In a large bowl, combine cooked brown rice, shelled edamame, diced red bell pepper, grated carrot, sliced green onions, chopped cilantro, chopped mint, and toasted sesame seeds.

3. **Toss with Dressing:**

   - Pour the dressing over the salad and toss everything together until well coated.

4. **Chill and Serve:**

   - Refrigerate the salad for at least 30 minutes before serving.

   - Serve chilled.

Nutritional Information (Per Serving):

- Calories: 280

- Protein: 9g

- Carbohydrates: 45g

- Fiber: 6g

- Sugars: 5g

- Fat: 8g

- Saturated Fat: 1g

- Cholesterol: 0mg

- Sodium: 420mg

- Vitamin C: 80% DV

- Vitamin A: 70% DV

- Iron: 15% DV

Summary:

This Edamame and Brown Rice Salad is a refreshing and nutritious dish that's loaded with fiber and plant-based protein. It's dressed with a zesty ginger-lime dressing and packed with vibrant flavors.

Tips and Tricks:

- Add your choice of protein (e.g., grilled chicken, tofu) to make it a complete meal.

- Customize with your favorite vegetables or herbs.

Ingredient Substitutions:

- Use quinoa instead of brown rice for a gluten-free option.

Chickpea and Spinach Curry

Ingredients:

- 2 (15-ounce) cans chickpeas, drained and rinsed

- 1 onion, finely chopped

- 2 cloves garlic, minced

- 1 tablespoon olive oil

- 2 tablespoons curry powder

- 1 teaspoon ground cumin

- 1/2 teaspoon ground coriander

- 1/2 teaspoon ground turmeric

- 1/4 teaspoon cayenne pepper (adjust to taste)

- 1 (14-ounce) can diced tomatoes

- 1 (14-ounce) can coconut milk

- 4 cups fresh spinach leaves

- Salt and pepper, to taste

- Cooked brown rice or naan bread, for serving

Instructions:

1. **Cook the Onion and Garlic:**

   - In a large skillet, heat olive oil over medium heat.

   - Add finely chopped onion and sauté for about 5 minutes until softened.

   - Add minced garlic and sauté for an additional minute until fragrant.

2. **Add the Spices:**

   - Stir in curry powder, ground cumin, ground coriander, ground turmeric, and cayenne pepper. Cook for another minute to toast the spices.

3. **Simmer the Sauce:**

   - Add diced tomatoes (with their juice) to the skillet.

   - Pour in coconut milk and stir to combine.

   - Simmer for about 10 minutes until the sauce thickens slightly.

4. **Add Chickpeas and Spinach:**

   - Stir in chickpeas and fresh spinach leaves.

- Cook for an additional 5-7 minutes until the spinach wilts and chickpeas are heated through.

5. **Season and Serve:**

   - Season with salt and pepper.
   - Serve the Chickpea and Spinach Curry over cooked brown rice or with naan bread.

Nutritional Information (Per Serving):

- Calories: 320
- Protein: 10g
- Carbohydrates: 38g
- Fiber: 9g
- Sugars: 5g
- Fat: 16g
- Saturated Fat: 10g
- Cholesterol: 0mg
- Sodium: 400mg
- Vitamin C: 20% DV

- Vitamin A: 70% DV

- Iron: 20% DV

Summary:

This Chickpea and Spinach Curry is a flavorful and protein-rich vegetarian dish. It's made with chickpeas, fresh spinach, and a fragrant blend of spices, all simmered in a creamy coconut tomato sauce.

Tips and Tricks:

- Adjust the level of spiciness by varying the amount of cayenne pepper.

- Customize with your favorite veggies or tofu.

Ingredient Substitutions:

- Use other leafy greens like kale or Swiss chard instead of spinach.

Turkey and Black Bean Tacos

Ingredients:

- 1 pound ground turkey

- 1 (15-ounce) can black beans, drained and rinsed

- 1 small onion, diced

- 2 cloves garlic, minced

- 1 tablespoon olive oil

- 2 tablespoons taco seasoning (store-bought or homemade)

- 1 cup diced tomatoes

- 1/2 cup shredded lettuce

- 1/2 cup diced red bell pepper

- 1/2 cup shredded cheddar cheese

- 8 small whole wheat tortillas

- Salsa and sliced avocado, for garnish (optional)

Instructions:

1. **Cook the Turkey and Beans:**

- In a large skillet, heat olive oil over medium-high heat.

- Add diced onion and minced garlic, and sauté for about 3-5 minutes until softened.

- Add ground turkey and cook until browned, breaking it into crumbles as it cooks.

- Stir in taco seasoning and cook for an additional 2-3 minutes.

- Add black beans and diced tomatoes to the skillet, and simmer for another 5 minutes until heated through.

2. **Assemble the Tacos:**

- Warm the whole wheat tortillas.

- Spoon the turkey and black bean mixture onto each tortilla.

3. **Add Toppings:**

- Top with shredded lettuce, diced red bell pepper, and shredded cheddar cheese.

4. **Garnish and Serve:**

- Garnish with salsa and sliced avocado if desired.

- Fold the tortillas and serve.

Nutritional Information (Per Serving, 2 Tacos):

- Calories: 350

- Protein: 25g

- Carbohydrates: 35g

- Fiber: 9g

- Sugars: 4g

- Fat: 13g

- Saturated Fat: 5g

- Cholesterol: 60mg

- Sodium: 550mg

- Vitamin C: 45% DV

- Vitamin A: 25% DV

- Iron: 20% DV

Summary:

These Turkey and Black Bean Tacos are a protein-packed and satisfying meal option. With seasoned ground turkey, black beans, and plenty of fresh toppings, they're a delicious and healthy choice for lunch or dinner.

Tips and Tricks:

- Customize with your favorite taco toppings like sour cream, guacamole, or hot sauce.

- Use ground chicken or beef instead of turkey if preferred.

Ingredient Substitutions:

- Substitute corn tortillas for whole wheat tortillas for a gluten-free option.

Spicy Tofu Stir-Fry

Ingredients:

- 1 block extra-firm tofu, pressed and cubed

- 2 cups broccoli florets

- 1 red bell pepper, sliced

- 1 carrot, thinly sliced

- 1/4 cup low-sodium soy sauce

- 2 tablespoons rice vinegar

- 2 tablespoons maple syrup or honey

- 1 tablespoon Sriracha sauce (adjust to taste)

- 1 tablespoon cornstarch

- 2 cloves garlic, minced

- 1 tablespoon grated fresh ginger

- 2 tablespoons sesame oil

- Cooked brown rice or quinoa, for serving

- Sesame seeds and sliced green onions, for garnish

Instructions:

1. **Prepare the Sauce:**

   - In a small bowl, whisk together low-sodium soy sauce, rice vinegar, maple syrup (or honey), Sriracha sauce, cornstarch, minced garlic, and grated fresh ginger. Set aside.

2. **Stir-Fry the Tofu:**

   - Heat sesame oil in a large skillet or wok over medium-high heat.

   - Add cubed tofu and cook until golden brown on all sides.

   - Remove the tofu from the skillet and set it aside.

3. **Stir-Fry the Vegetables:**

   - In the same skillet, add broccoli florets, sliced red bell pepper, and thinly sliced carrot.

   - Stir-fry for about 5-7 minutes until the vegetables are tender-crisp.

4. **Combine and Add Sauce:**

- Return the cooked tofu to the skillet with the stir-fried vegetables.

- Pour the sauce over the tofu and vegetables.

- Stir to coat everything evenly with the sauce.

- Cook for an additional 2-3 minutes until the sauce thickens.

5. **Serve:**

- Serve the Spicy Tofu Stir-Fry over cooked brown rice or quinoa.

- Garnish with sesame seeds and sliced green onions.

Nutritional Information (Per Serving):

- Calories: 320

- Protein: 18g

- Carbohydrates: 40g

- Fiber: 5g

- Sugars: 14g

- Fat: 11g

- Saturated Fat: 2g

- Cholesterol: 0mg

- Sodium: 780mg

- Vitamin C: 140% DV

- Vitamin A: 80% DV

- Iron: 15% DV

Summary:

This Spicy Tofu Stir-Fry is a protein-rich and flavorful dish that combines crispy tofu with a variety of colorful vegetables and a spicy sauce. It's a quick and satisfying option for a healthy lunch or dinner.

Tips and Tricks:

- Adjust the level of spiciness by varying the amount of Sriracha sauce.

- Add cashews or peanuts for extra crunch.

Ingredient Substitutions:

- Use tempeh or seitan as a substitute for tofu.

Salmon and Quinoa Bowl

Ingredients:

- 2 salmon fillets

- 1 cup quinoa, rinsed and drained

- 2 cups low-sodium vegetable broth

- 2 cups mixed greens

- 1 cup cherry tomatoes, halved

- 1/2 cucumber, diced

- 1/4 cup red onion, finely chopped

- 1/4 cup fresh parsley, chopped

- Juice of 1 lemon

- 2 tablespoons olive oil

- Salt and pepper, to taste

Instructions:

1. **Cook the Quinoa:**

   - In a medium saucepan, bring the vegetable broth to a boil.

- Add quinoa, reduce heat to low, cover, and simmer for about 15-20 minutes, or until all liquid is absorbed and quinoa is tender.

- Remove from heat, fluff with a fork, and let it cool.

2. **Prepare the Salmon:**

- Season the salmon fillets with salt and pepper.

- Heat olive oil in a skillet over medium-high heat.

- Add salmon fillets and cook for about 4-5 minutes per side until they are cooked through and flake easily with a fork.

3. **Assemble the Bowl:**

- In a large bowl, combine the cooked quinoa, mixed greens, cherry tomatoes, diced cucumber, chopped red onion, and fresh parsley.

4. **Make the Dressing:**

- In a small bowl, whisk together lemon juice, olive oil, salt, and pepper.

5. **Drizzle and Serve:**

   - Drizzle the dressing over the bowl and gently toss everything together to combine.

   - Top the salad with the cooked salmon fillets.

Nutritional Information (Per Serving):

- Calories: 400

- Protein: 30g

- Carbohydrates: 35g

- Fiber: 5g

- Sugars: 4g

- Fat: 15g

- Saturated Fat: 2.5g

- Cholesterol: 60mg

- Sodium: 350mg

- Vitamin C: 45% DV

- Vitamin A: 25% DV

- Iron: 20% DV

Summary:

This Salmon and Quinoa Bowl is a protein-packed and nutritious meal that combines perfectly cooked salmon with quinoa, fresh vegetables, and a zesty lemon dressing. It's a satisfying option for a healthy lunch or dinner.

Tips and Tricks:

- Customize the bowl with your favorite veggies or herbs.

- Substitute other types of fish like trout or tilapia if preferred.

Ingredient Substitutions:

- Use brown rice instead of quinoa for a different grain option.

Blackened Chicken Salad

Ingredients:

- 2 boneless, skinless chicken breasts
- 2 teaspoons paprika
- 1 teaspoon dried thyme
- 1/2 teaspoon garlic powder
- 1/2 teaspoon onion powder
- 1/2 teaspoon cayenne pepper
- Salt and black pepper, to taste
- 2 tablespoons olive oil
- 4 cups mixed salad greens
- 1 cup cherry tomatoes, halved
- 1/2 cucumber, sliced
- 1/4 cup red onion, thinly sliced
- 1/4 cup sliced black olives
- 1/4 cup crumbled feta cheese
- Balsamic vinaigrette dressing, for serving

Instructions:

1. **Season the Chicken:**

   - In a small bowl, combine paprika, dried thyme, garlic powder, onion powder, cayenne pepper, salt, and black pepper.

   - Rub the spice mixture evenly over both sides of the chicken breasts.

2. **Cook the Chicken:**

   - Heat olive oil in a skillet over medium-high heat.

   - Add chicken breasts and cook for about 5-7 minutes per side until they are cooked through and no longer pink in the center.

   - Remove the chicken from the skillet and let it rest for a few minutes before slicing.

3. **Assemble the Salad:**

   - In a large salad bowl, arrange mixed salad greens, cherry tomatoes, sliced cucumber, thinly sliced red onion, sliced black olives, and crumbled feta cheese.

4. **Add Chicken and Dressing:**

   - Top the salad with sliced blackened chicken breasts.

   - Drizzle with balsamic vinaigrette dressing.

Nutritional Information (Per Serving):

- Calories: 350

- Protein: 30g

- Carbohydrates: 12g

- Fiber: 3g

- Sugars: 5g

- Fat: 18g

- Saturated Fat: 5g

- Cholesterol: 85mg

- Sodium: 550mg

- Vitamin C: 40% DV

- Vitamin A: 30% DV

- Iron: 15% DV

Summary:

This Blackened Chicken Salad is a protein-rich and flavorful meal that features blackened chicken breasts served on a bed of mixed greens with cherry tomatoes, cucumber, red onion, olives, and feta cheese. It's a satisfying and healthy lunch option.

Tips and Tricks:

- Adjust the level of spiciness by varying the amount of cayenne pepper.

- Customize the salad with your favorite veggies and dressing.

Ingredient Substitutions:

- Use grilled shrimp or tofu as a protein alternative to chicken.

Lentil and Mushroom Stuffed Bell Peppers

Ingredients:

- 4 large bell peppers, any color
- 1 cup green or brown lentils, rinsed and drained
- 2 cups low-sodium vegetable broth
- 1 onion, finely chopped
- 2 cloves garlic, minced
- 1 cup mushrooms, finely chopped
- 1/2 cup diced tomatoes (canned or fresh)
- 1 teaspoon dried oregano
- 1/2 teaspoon dried basil
- Salt and black pepper, to taste
- Olive oil, for cooking
- Grated Parmesan cheese, for garnish (optional)
- Fresh parsley, for garnish

Instructions:

1. **Prepare the Bell Peppers:**

   - Cut the tops off the bell peppers and remove the seeds and membranes from the inside.

   - If needed, trim the bottoms of the peppers slightly to make them stand upright.

2. **Cook the Lentils:**

   - In a saucepan, combine lentils and vegetable broth.

   - Bring to a boil, then reduce heat to low, cover, and simmer for about 20-25 minutes, or until lentils are tender and liquid is absorbed.

3. **Prepare the Filling:**

   - In a skillet, heat olive oil over medium-high heat.

   - Add finely chopped onion and minced garlic. Sauté for about 3-5 minutes until softened.

   - Add finely chopped mushrooms, diced tomatoes, dried oregano, dried basil, salt, and black pepper. Cook for an additional 5-7 minutes until mushrooms are tender and any liquid has evaporated.

4. **Combine Lentils and Mushroom Mixture:**

   - Stir the cooked lentils into the mushroom mixture. Remove from heat.

5. **Stuff the Bell Peppers:**

   - Preheat your oven to 350°F (175°C).

   - Fill each bell pepper with the lentil and mushroom mixture, pressing it down gently.

6. **Bake:**

   - Place the stuffed bell peppers in a baking dish.

   - Cover the dish with aluminum foil and bake for about 25-30 minutes, or until the peppers are tender.

7. **Serve:**

   - Garnish with grated Parmesan cheese (optional) and fresh parsley.

   - Serve hot.

Nutritional Information (Per Serving, 1 Stuffed Bell Pepper):

- Calories: 250

- Protein: 13g

- Carbohydrates: 48g

- Fiber: 14g

- Sugars: 9g

- Fat: 2g

- Saturated Fat: 0g

- Cholesterol: 0mg

- Sodium: 390mg

- Vitamin C: 380% DV

- Vitamin A: 90% DV

- Iron: 15% DV

Summary:

These Lentil and Mushroom Stuffed Bell Peppers are a protein-packed and nutritious option for a satisfying meal. Lentils and mushrooms create a flavorful and hearty filling, and the peppers add a vibrant touch.

Tips and Tricks:

- Customize the filling with your favorite herbs, spices, or veggies.

- Use quinoa or rice as a substitute for lentils if preferred.

Ingredient Substitutions:

- Use any type of bell peppers you prefer or have on hand.

Tuna and White Bean Salad

Ingredients:

- 2 (5-ounce) cans of tuna in water, drained
- 2 (15-ounce) cans of cannellini beans, drained and rinsed
- 1/4 cup red onion, finely chopped
- 1/4 cup diced celery
- 1/4 cup diced red bell pepper
- 2 tablespoons chopped fresh parsley
- 1/4 cup olive oil
- 2 tablespoons red wine vinegar
- 1 teaspoon Dijon mustard
- Salt and black pepper, to taste
- Lemon wedges, for garnish (optional)

Instructions:

1. **Prepare the Salad:**

- In a large bowl, combine drained tuna, cannellini beans, finely chopped red onion, diced celery, diced red bell pepper, and chopped fresh parsley.

2. **Make the Dressing:**

   - In a small bowl, whisk together olive oil, red wine vinegar, Dijon mustard, salt, and black pepper.

3. **Toss and Chill:**

   - Pour the dressing over the salad ingredients.

   - Gently toss everything together until well coated.

   - Refrigerate the salad for about 30 minutes to allow the flavors to meld.

4. **Serve:**

   - Serve the Tuna and White Bean Salad with lemon wedges for garnish, if desired.

Nutritional Information (Per Serving):

- Calories: 320

- Protein: 27g

- Carbohydrates: 24g

- Fiber: 7g

- Sugars: 2g

- Fat: 14g

- Saturated Fat: 2g

- Cholesterol: 30mg

- Sodium: 520mg

- Vitamin C: 20% DV

- Vitamin A: 15% DV

- Iron: 20% DV

Summary:

This Tuna and White Bean Salad is a protein-rich and flavorful dish that's perfect for a quick and nutritious lunch or dinner. It combines canned tuna, cannellini beans, and a zesty dressing for a satisfying meal.

Tips and Tricks:

- Customize with your favorite herbs, such as basil or dill.

- Serve over mixed greens or on whole wheat bread as a sandwich.

Ingredient Substitutions:

- Use canned salmon or cooked chicken as a substitute for tuna.

Shrimp and Avocado Salad

Ingredients:

- 1 pound large shrimp, peeled and deveined

- 2 avocados, diced

- 1 cup cherry tomatoes, halved

- 1/4 cup red onion, finely chopped

- 2 tablespoons fresh cilantro, chopped

- Juice of 2 limes

- 2 tablespoons olive oil

- Salt and black pepper, to taste

- Mixed salad greens, for serving

Instructions:

1. **Cook the Shrimp:**

    - Season shrimp with salt and black pepper.

    - In a skillet, heat olive oil over medium-high heat.

- Add shrimp and cook for about 2-3 minutes per side until they are pink and cooked through.

2. **Prepare the Salad:**

   - In a large bowl, combine diced avocados, halved cherry tomatoes, finely chopped red onion, and chopped fresh cilantro.

3. **Make the Dressing:**

   - In a small bowl, whisk together lime juice and olive oil.

   - Season with salt and black pepper.

4. **Combine and Serve:**

   - Add the cooked shrimp to the salad ingredients.

   - Drizzle the dressing over the salad and gently toss to combine.

   - Serve over mixed salad greens.

Nutritional Information (Per Serving):

- Calories: 320

- Protein: 24g

- Carbohydrates: 16g

- Fiber: 8g

- Sugars: 3g

- Fat: 20g

- Saturated Fat: 3g

- Cholesterol: 175mg

- Sodium: 200mg

- Vitamin C: 30% DV

- Vitamin A: 15% DV

- Iron: 15% DV

Summary:

This Shrimp and Avocado Salad is a protein-packed and refreshing dish that combines succulent shrimp with creamy avocado and zesty lime dressing. It's a perfect option for a light and healthy lunch.

Tips and Tricks:

- Customize with your favorite herbs or add a touch of heat with diced jalapeños.

- Serve with a side of crusty whole wheat bread.

Ingredient Substitutions:

- Use cooked chicken or tofu as a substitute for shrimp.

Quinoa and Black Bean Stuffed Peppers

Ingredients:

- 4 large bell peppers, any color
- 1 cup quinoa, rinsed and drained
- 2 cups low-sodium vegetable broth
- 1 (15-ounce) can black beans, drained and rinsed
- 1 cup diced tomatoes (canned or fresh)
- 1/2 cup corn kernels (fresh or frozen)
- 1/4 cup red onion, finely chopped
- 1 teaspoon chili powder
- 1/2 teaspoon ground cumin
- Salt and black pepper, to taste
- Shredded cheddar cheese, for garnish (optional)
- Fresh cilantro, for garnish

Instructions:

1. **Prepare the Bell Peppers:**

- Cut the tops off the bell peppers and remove the seeds and membranes from the inside.

- If needed, trim the bottoms of the peppers slightly to make them stand upright.

2. **Cook the Quinoa:**

- In a saucepan, bring the vegetable broth to a boil.

- Add quinoa, reduce heat to low, cover, and simmer for about 15-20 minutes, or until all liquid is absorbed and quinoa is tender.

- Remove from heat and let it cool.

3. **Prepare the Filling:**

- In a large bowl, combine cooked quinoa, black beans, diced tomatoes, corn kernels, finely chopped red onion, chili powder, ground cumin, salt, and black pepper.

4. **Stuff the Bell Peppers:**

- Preheat your oven to 350°F (175°C).

- Fill each bell pepper with the quinoa and black bean mixture, pressing it down gently.

5. **Bake:**

   - Place the stuffed bell peppers in a baking dish.

   - Cover the dish with aluminum foil and bake for about 25-30 minutes, or until the peppers are tender.

6. **Serve:**

   - Garnish with shredded cheddar cheese (optional) and fresh cilantro.

   - Serve hot.

Nutritional Information (Per Serving, 1 Stuffed Bell Pepper):

- Calories: 300

- Protein: 11g

- Carbohydrates: 55g

- Fiber: 11g

- Sugars: 8g

- Fat: 4g

- Saturated Fat: 1g

- Cholesterol: 0mg

- Sodium: 490mg

- Vitamin C: 240% DV

- Vitamin A: 100% DV

- Iron: 20% DV

Summary:

These Quinoa and Black Bean Stuffed Peppers are a nutritious and satisfying meal that combines fluffy quinoa, black beans, corn, and tomatoes, all stuffed into bell peppers and baked to perfection.

Tips and Tricks:

- Customize the filling with your favorite spices or add diced jalapeños for extra heat.

- Drizzle with hot sauce or salsa before serving.

Ingredient Substitutions:

- Use brown rice instead of quinoa for a different grain option.

Turkey and Spinach Meatballs

Ingredients:

- 1 pound ground turkey
- 1 cup fresh spinach leaves, finely chopped
- 1/4 cup grated Parmesan cheese
- 1/4 cup breadcrumbs (whole wheat or gluten-free)
- 1/4 cup diced red onion
- 1 clove garlic, minced
- 1 teaspoon dried oregano
- 1/2 teaspoon dried basil
- Salt and black pepper, to taste
- Olive oil, for cooking
- Marinara sauce, for serving

Instructions:

1. **Prepare the Meatball Mixture:**

- In a large bowl, combine ground turkey, finely chopped fresh spinach, grated Parmesan cheese, breadcrumbs, diced red onion, minced garlic, dried oregano, dried basil, salt, and black pepper.

- Mix until all ingredients are well combined.

2. **Form Meatballs:**

- Shape the mixture into meatballs, about 1-2 inches in diameter.

3. **Cook the Meatballs:**

- Heat olive oil in a skillet over medium-high heat.

- Add the meatballs and cook for about 6-8 minutes, turning frequently, until they are browned on all sides and cooked through.

4. **Serve:**

- Serve the Turkey and Spinach Meatballs with marinara sauce for dipping.

Nutritional Information (Per Serving, 4 Meatballs):

- Calories: 250

- Protein: 25g

- Carbohydrates: 6g

- Fiber: 1g

- Sugars: 1g

- Fat: 15g

- Saturated Fat: 4g

- Cholesterol: 70mg

- Sodium: 450mg

- Vitamin C: 4% DV

- Vitamin A: 15% DV

- Iron: 15% DV

Summary:

These Turkey and Spinach Meatballs are a protein-packed and flavorful option for a healthy lunch or dinner. They are made with ground turkey, fresh spinach, and Italian seasonings, and can be served with marinara sauce for extra flavor.

Tips and Tricks:

- Customize the meatball mixture with your favorite herbs or spices.

- Serve over whole wheat pasta or zucchini noodles for a complete meal.

Ingredient Substitutions:

- Use ground chicken or lean ground beef instead of turkey.

Veggie and Tofu Stir-Fry

Ingredients:

- 1 block extra-firm tofu, pressed and cubed
- 2 cups broccoli florets
- 1 red bell pepper, sliced
- 1 yellow bell pepper, sliced
- 1 carrot, thinly sliced
- 1/2 cup snow peas
- 1/4 cup low-sodium soy sauce
- 2 tablespoons rice vinegar
- 2 tablespoons honey or maple syrup
- 1 tablespoon cornstarch
- 2 cloves garlic, minced
- 1 tablespoon grated fresh ginger
- 2 tablespoons vegetable oil
- Cooked brown rice or quinoa, for serving
- Sesame seeds and sliced green onions, for garnish

Instructions:

1. **Prepare the Sauce:**

    - In a small bowl, whisk together low-sodium soy sauce, rice vinegar, honey (or maple syrup), cornstarch, minced garlic, and grated fresh ginger. Set aside.

2. **Stir-Fry the Tofu:**

    - Heat vegetable oil in a large skillet or wok over medium-high heat.

    - Add cubed tofu and cook until golden brown on all sides.

    - Remove the tofu from the skillet and set it aside.

3. **Stir-Fry the Vegetables:**

    - In the same skillet, add broccoli florets, sliced red bell pepper, sliced yellow bell pepper, thinly sliced carrot, and snow peas.

    - Stir-fry for about 5-7 minutes until the vegetables are tender-crisp.

4. **Combine and Add Sauce:**

- Return the cooked tofu to the skillet with the stir-fried vegetables.

- Pour the sauce over the tofu and vegetables.

- Stir to coat everything evenly with the sauce.

- Cook for an additional 2-3 minutes until the sauce thickens.

5. **Serve:**

- Serve the Veggie and Tofu Stir-Fry over cooked brown rice or quinoa.

- Garnish with sesame seeds and sliced green onions.

Nutritional Information (Per Serving):

- Calories: 320

- Protein: 16g

- Carbohydrates: 42g

- Fiber: 6g

- Sugars: 14g

- Fat: 12g

- Saturated Fat: 1.5g

- Cholesterol: 0mg

- Sodium: 800mg

- Vitamin C: 260% DV

- Vitamin A: 120% DV

- Iron: 20% DV

Summary:

This Veggie and Tofu Stir-Fry is a protein-rich and colorful dish that combines crispy tofu with a variety of vibrant vegetables and a savory-sweet sauce. It's a quick and satisfying option for a healthy lunch or dinner.

Tips and Tricks:

- Customize with your favorite veggies or add cashews for extra crunch.

- Adjust the sauce sweetness to taste by varying the amount of honey or maple syrup.

Ingredient Substitutions:

- Use tempeh or seitan as a substitute for tofu.

Grilled Salmon with Asparagus

Ingredients:

- 2 salmon fillets
- 1 bunch asparagus, trimmed
- 2 tablespoons olive oil
- 1 lemon, thinly sliced
- 2 cloves garlic, minced
- 1 teaspoon dried thyme
- Salt and black pepper, to taste
- Fresh dill, for garnish (optional)

Instructions:

1. **Preheat the Grill:**

   - Preheat your grill to medium-high heat.

2. **Prepare the Salmon and Asparagus:**

   - Brush salmon fillets and trimmed asparagus with olive oil.

- Season with minced garlic, dried thyme, salt, and black pepper.
- Place lemon slices on top of the salmon fillets.

3. **Grill:**

- Place the salmon fillets and asparagus directly on the grill grates.
- Grill the salmon for about 4-5 minutes per side until they are cooked through and flake easily with a fork.
- Grill the asparagus for about 5-7 minutes until they are tender-crisp and have grill marks.

4. **Serve:**

- Transfer the grilled salmon and asparagus to a serving platter.
- Garnish with fresh dill if desired.
- Serve hot.

Nutritional Information (Per Serving):

- Calories: 350

- Protein: 30g

- Carbohydrates: 8g

- Fiber: 3g

- Sugars: 2g

- Fat: 22g

- Saturated Fat: 4g

- Cholesterol: 75mg

- Sodium: 110mg

- Vitamin C: 35% DV

- Vitamin A: 20% DV

- Iron: 15% DV

Summary:

This Grilled Salmon with Asparagus is a protein-rich and delicious dish that's perfect for a healthy lunch or dinner. The salmon is seasoned and grilled to perfection alongside tender-crisp asparagus.

Tips and Tricks:

- Use a grill basket or foil to prevent asparagus from falling through grill grates.

- Serve with a side of quinoa or a fresh salad.

Ingredient Substitutions:

- Substitute other types of fish like trout or tilapia if preferred.

Chickpea and Quinoa Salad

Ingredients:

- 1 cup quinoa, rinsed and drained
- 2 cups low-sodium vegetable broth
- 1 (15-ounce) can chickpeas, drained and rinsed
- 1 cup cherry tomatoes, halved
- 1 cucumber, diced
- 1/4 cup red onion, finely chopped
- 1/4 cup fresh parsley, chopped
- Juice of 1 lemon
- 2 tablespoons olive oil
- Salt and black pepper, to taste

Instructions:

1. **Cook the Quinoa:**

   - In a medium saucepan, bring the vegetable broth to a boil.

- Add quinoa, reduce heat to low, cover, and simmer for about 15-20 minutes, or until all liquid is absorbed and quinoa is tender.

- Remove from heat, fluff with a fork, and let it cool.

2. **Prepare the Salad:**

- In a large bowl, combine cooked quinoa, chickpeas, halved cherry tomatoes, diced cucumber, finely chopped red onion, and chopped fresh parsley.

3. **Make the Dressing:**

- In a small bowl, whisk together lemon juice and olive oil.

- Season with salt and black pepper.

4. **Toss and Serve:**

- Drizzle the dressing over the salad ingredients.

- Gently toss everything together until well coated.

- Serve chilled.

Nutritional Information (Per Serving):

- Calories: 300

- Protein: 10g

- Carbohydrates: 50g

- Fiber: 8g

- Sugars: 4g

- Fat: 7g

- Saturated Fat: 1g

- Cholesterol: 0mg

- Sodium: 350mg

- Vitamin C: 40% DV

- Vitamin A: 15% DV

- Iron: 20% DV

Summary:

This Chickpea and Quinoa Salad is a protein-packed and nutritious dish that combines quinoa, chickpeas, fresh vegetables, and a zesty lemon dressing. It's a satisfying and healthy lunch or side dish.

Tips and Tricks:

- Customize the salad with your favorite herbs or add feta cheese for extra flavor.

- Add grilled chicken or tofu for additional protein.

Ingredient Substitutions:

- Use couscous or bulgur as a substitute for quinoa.

Greek Yogurt Chicken Salad

Ingredients:

- 2 cups cooked chicken breast, diced
- 1/2 cup Greek yogurt (non-fat or low-fat)
- 1/4 cup diced celery
- 1/4 cup diced red onion
- 1/4 cup diced red grapes
- 1/4 cup chopped walnuts
- 1 tablespoon Dijon mustard
- 1 tablespoon honey
- 1 tablespoon lemon juice
- Salt and black pepper, to taste
- Mixed salad greens or whole wheat bread, for serving

Instructions:

1. **Prepare the Dressing:**

- In a small bowl, whisk together Greek yogurt, Dijon mustard, honey, lemon juice, salt, and black pepper.

2. **Combine Ingredients:**

   - In a large bowl, combine diced chicken breast, diced celery, diced red onion, diced red grapes, and chopped walnuts.

3. **Add Dressing:**

   - Pour the dressing over the chicken salad mixture.

   - Gently toss everything together until well coated.

4. **Serve:**

   - Serve the Greek Yogurt Chicken Salad on a bed of mixed salad greens or as a sandwich on whole wheat bread.

Nutritional Information (Per Serving):

- Calories: 320

- Protein: 30g

- Carbohydrates: 20g

- Fiber: 3g

- Sugars: 15g

- Fat: 15g

- Saturated Fat: 2g

- Cholesterol: 65mg

- Sodium: 280mg

- Vitamin C: 6% DV

- Vitamin A: 4% DV

- Iron: 10% DV

Summary:

This Greek Yogurt Chicken Salad is a protein-rich and creamy dish that's perfect for a quick and healthy lunch. It combines diced chicken breast with Greek yogurt, grapes, celery, and walnuts for a delightful combination of flavors and textures.

Tips and Tricks:

- Customize with your favorite fruits or add a pinch of dried herbs for extra flavor.

- Serve over mixed greens or as a sandwich.

Ingredient Substitutions:

- Use turkey or tofu as a substitute for chicken.

Spinach and Feta Stuffed Chicken

Ingredients:

- 2 boneless, skinless chicken breasts
- 2 cups fresh spinach leaves
- 1/2 cup crumbled feta cheese
- 2 cloves garlic, minced
- 1 teaspoon dried oregano
- Salt and black pepper, to taste
- Olive oil, for cooking
- Lemon wedges, for serving (optional)

Instructions:

1. **Prepare the Chicken:**

   - Slice each chicken breast horizontally to create a pocket without cutting all the way through.
   - Season the inside and outside of the chicken breasts with salt and black pepper.

2. **Stuff the Chicken:**

- Stuff each chicken breast with fresh spinach leaves, crumbled feta cheese, minced garlic, and dried oregano.

- Secure the open ends with toothpicks.

3. **Cook the Chicken:**

   - Heat olive oil in an ovenproof skillet over medium-high heat.

   - Add stuffed chicken breasts and sear for about 2-3 minutes per side until they are golden brown.

4. **Bake:**

   - Preheat your oven to 375°F (190°C).

   - Transfer the skillet to the preheated oven and bake for about 20-25 minutes, or until the chicken is cooked through and no longer pink in the center.

5. **Serve:**

   - Remove toothpicks before serving.

   - Serve the Spinach and Feta Stuffed Chicken with lemon wedges if desired.

Nutritional Information (Per Serving):

- Calories: 350
- Protein: 40g
- Carbohydrates: 3g
- Fiber: 1g
- Sugars: 1g
- Fat: 18g
- Saturated Fat: 7g
- Cholesterol: 120mg
- Sodium: 450mg
- Vitamin C: 10% DV
- Vitamin A: 30% DV
- Iron: 15% DV

Summary:

This Spinach and Feta Stuffed Chicken is a protein-rich and flavorful dish that features tender chicken breasts stuffed with spinach and feta cheese. It's an elegant and satisfying option for a healthy lunch or dinner.

Tips and Tricks:

- Customize the stuffing with your favorite herbs or add diced sun-dried tomatoes.

- Serve with a side of quinoa or a fresh salad.

Ingredient Substitutions:

- Use goat cheese or mozzarella cheese as a substitute for feta.

Tofu and Vegetable Skewers

Ingredients:

- 1 block extra-firm tofu, pressed and cubed
- 1 red bell pepper, cut into chunks
- 1 yellow bell pepper, cut into chunks
- 1 zucchini, sliced into rounds
- 1 red onion, cut into chunks
- 1/4 cup olive oil
- 2 tablespoons balsamic vinegar
- 1 teaspoon dried Italian seasoning
- Salt and black pepper, to taste
- Wooden skewers, soaked in water

Instructions:

1. **Prepare the Marinade:**

   - In a small bowl, whisk together olive oil, balsamic vinegar, dried Italian seasoning, salt, and black pepper.

2. **Assemble the Skewers:**

   - Thread cubed tofu, red bell pepper chunks, yellow bell pepper chunks, zucchini rounds, and red onion chunks onto the soaked wooden skewers, alternating the ingredients.

3. **Marinate:**

   - Place the skewers in a shallow dish and pour the marinade over them.

   - Let them marinate for at least 30 minutes, turning occasionally.

4. **Grill:**

   - Preheat your grill to medium-high heat.

   - Grill the tofu and vegetable skewers for about 8-10 minutes, turning occasionally, until they are lightly charred and the tofu is heated through.

5. **Serve:**

   - Remove from the grill and serve hot.

Nutritional Information (Per Serving, 2 Skewers):

- Calories: 280

- Protein: 10g

- Carbohydrates: 14g

- Fiber: 3g

- Sugars: 7g

- Fat: 20g

- Saturated Fat: 3g

- Cholesterol: 0mg

- Sodium: 60mg

- Vitamin C: 170% DV

- Vitamin A: 15% DV

- Iron: 10% DV

Summary:

These Tofu and Vegetable Skewers are a protein-packed and flavorful option for a healthy lunch or dinner. The tofu and veggies are marinated and grilled to perfection, making them a great addition to your meal.

Tips and Tricks:

- Customize with your favorite vegetables or add a drizzle of tahini sauce.

- Serve over cooked quinoa or brown rice for a complete meal.

Ingredient Substitutions:

- Use tempeh or seitan as a substitute for tofu.

Lentil and Sweet Potato Curry

Ingredients:

- 1 cup dried green or brown lentils, rinsed and drained

- 2 large sweet potatoes, peeled and diced

- 1 onion, finely chopped

- 3 cloves garlic, minced

- 1-inch piece of fresh ginger, grated

- 2 tablespoons curry powder

- 1 teaspoon ground cumin

- 1 teaspoon ground coriander

- 1/2 teaspoon ground turmeric

- 1/4 teaspoon cayenne pepper (adjust to taste)

- 1 (14-ounce) can diced tomatoes

- 1 (14-ounce) can coconut milk

- 2 cups vegetable broth

- Salt and black pepper, to taste

- Fresh cilantro, for garnish (optional)

- Cooked brown rice or naan bread, for serving

Instructions:

1. **Sauté Onion and Garlic:**

   - In a large pot or Dutch oven, heat a bit of vegetable broth or oil over medium heat.

   - Add chopped onion and sauté for about 3-5 minutes until translucent.

   - Add minced garlic and grated ginger and cook for an additional 1-2 minutes until fragrant.

2. **Add Spices and Sweet Potatoes:**

   - Stir in curry powder, ground cumin, ground coriander, ground turmeric, and cayenne pepper.

   - Add diced sweet potatoes and cook for about 5 minutes, stirring occasionally.

3. **Add Lentils and Liquid:**

   - Add rinsed lentils, diced tomatoes, coconut milk, and vegetable broth to the pot.

- Season with salt and black pepper.
- Bring the mixture to a boil, then reduce heat to low, cover, and simmer for about 20-25 minutes, or until lentils and sweet potatoes are tender.

4. **Serve:**

- Serve the Lentil and Sweet Potato Curry hot, garnished with fresh cilantro if desired.
- Serve with cooked brown rice or naan bread.

Nutritional Information (Per Serving):

- Calories: 400
- Protein: 15g
- Carbohydrates: 58g
- Fiber: 14g
- Sugars: 10g
- Fat: 13g
- Saturated Fat: 10g
- Cholesterol: 0mg

- Sodium: 600mg

- Vitamin C: 40% DV

- Vitamin A: 320% DV

- Iron: 25% DV

Summary:

This Lentil and Sweet Potato Curry is a protein-rich and flavorful dish that combines lentils, sweet potatoes, and aromatic spices in a creamy coconut milk sauce. It's a comforting and satisfying meal for lunch or dinner.

Tips and Tricks:

- Adjust the level of spice by varying the amount of cayenne pepper.

- Customize with your favorite vegetables like spinach or bell peppers.

Ingredient Substitutions:

- Use red lentils or yellow lentils as a substitute for green or brown lentils.

Turkey and Black Bean Chili

Ingredients:

- 1 pound ground turkey
- 1 onion, chopped
- 3 cloves garlic, minced
- 1 bell pepper, diced
- 1 (15-ounce) can black beans, drained and rinsed
- 1 (14-ounce) can diced tomatoes
- 2 tablespoons chili powder
- 1 teaspoon ground cumin
- 1/2 teaspoon paprika
- 1/2 teaspoon cayenne pepper (adjust to taste)
- Salt and black pepper, to taste
- 2 cups low-sodium chicken broth
- Chopped fresh cilantro, for garnish (optional)
- Shredded cheddar cheese, for garnish (optional)
- Sour cream, for garnish (optional)

Instructions:

1. **Sauté Onion and Garlic:**

   - In a large pot or Dutch oven, heat a bit of olive oil over medium heat.

   - Add chopped onion and sauté for about 3-5 minutes until translucent.

   - Add minced garlic and cook for an additional 1-2 minutes until fragrant.

2. **Brown the Turkey:**

   - Add ground turkey to the pot and cook, breaking it apart with a spoon, until it's no longer pink.

3. **Add Vegetables and Spices:**

   - Stir in diced bell pepper, black beans, diced tomatoes, chili powder, ground cumin, paprika, cayenne pepper, salt, and black pepper.

4. **Simmer:**

   - Pour in low-sodium chicken broth and stir to combine.

- Bring the mixture to a boil, then reduce heat to low, cover, and simmer for about 30 minutes, stirring occasionally.

5. **Serve:**

- Serve the Turkey and Black Bean Chili hot, garnished with chopped fresh cilantro, shredded cheddar cheese, and sour cream if desired.

Nutritional Information (Per Serving):

- Calories: 350

- Protein: 25g

- Carbohydrates: 30g

- Fiber: 9g

- Sugars: 5g

- Fat: 14g

- Saturated Fat: 3g

- Cholesterol: 55mg

- Sodium: 600mg

- Vitamin C: 40% DV

- Vitamin A: 20% DV

- Iron: 20% DV

Summary:

This Turkey and Black Bean Chili is a protein-rich and hearty dish that combines ground turkey, black beans, and flavorful spices for a satisfying meal. It's perfect for a comforting lunch or dinner.

Tips and Tricks:

- Customize the level of spiciness by adjusting the amount of chili powder and cayenne pepper.

- Serve with a dollop of Greek yogurt instead of sour cream for added protein.

Ingredient Substitutions:

- Use ground beef or ground chicken as a substitute for ground turkey.

Quinoa and Chickpea Salad

Ingredients:

- 1 cup quinoa, rinsed and drained

- 2 cups water

- 1 (15-ounce) can chickpeas, drained and rinsed

- 1 cucumber, diced

- 1 red bell pepper, diced

- 1/4 cup red onion, finely chopped

- 1/4 cup fresh parsley, chopped

- Juice of 2 lemons

- 2 tablespoons olive oil

- Salt and black pepper, to taste

- Feta cheese, for garnish (optional)

Instructions:

1. **Cook the Quinoa:**

   - In a medium saucepan, bring water to a boil.

- Add quinoa, reduce heat to low, cover, and simmer for about 15-20 minutes, or until all liquid is absorbed and quinoa is tender.

- Remove from heat, fluff with a fork, and let it cool.

2. **Prepare the Salad:**

   - In a large bowl, combine cooked quinoa, chickpeas, diced cucumber, diced red bell pepper, finely chopped red onion, and chopped fresh parsley.

3. **Make the Dressing:**

   - In a small bowl, whisk together lemon juice, olive oil, salt, and black pepper.

4. **Toss and Serve:**

   - Drizzle the dressing over the salad ingredients.

   - Gently toss everything together until well coated.

   - Serve chilled, garnished with crumbled feta cheese if desired.

Nutritional Information (Per Serving):

- Calories: 320
- Protein: 10g
- Carbohydrates: 52g
- Fiber: 9g
- Sugars: 4g
- Fat: 10g
- Saturated Fat: 1.5g
- Cholesterol: 0mg
- Sodium: 390mg
- Vitamin C: 50% DV
- Vitamin A: 15% DV
- Iron: 20% DV

Summary:

This Quinoa and Chickpea Salad is a protein-packed and refreshing dish that combines fluffy quinoa, chickpeas, and a zesty lemon dressing. It's a perfect option for a light and healthy lunch.

Tips and Tricks:

- Customize with your favorite herbs or add olives and cherry tomatoes for extra flavor.

- Add grilled chicken or tofu for additional protein.

Ingredient Substitutions:

- Use couscous or bulgur as a substitute for quinoa.

Caprese Stuffed Portobello Mushrooms

Ingredients:

- 4 large portobello mushrooms, stems removed
- 1 cup cherry tomatoes, halved
- 1 cup fresh mozzarella balls (ciliegine)
- 1/4 cup fresh basil leaves, chopped
- 2 cloves garlic, minced
- 2 tablespoons balsamic vinegar
- 2 tablespoons olive oil
- Salt and black pepper, to taste
- Balsamic glaze, for drizzling
- Fresh basil leaves, for garnish

Instructions:

1. **Prepare the Mushrooms:**

   - Preheat your oven to 375°F (190°C).
   - Place portobello mushrooms on a baking sheet, gill side up.

- Drizzle with olive oil and season with salt and black pepper.

2. **Bake the Mushrooms:**

   - Bake the mushrooms in the preheated oven for about 12–15 minutes, or until they are tender.

3. **Prepare the Caprese Filling:**

   - In a bowl, combine cherry tomato halves, fresh mozzarella balls, chopped fresh basil, minced garlic, balsamic vinegar, and olive oil.

   - Season with salt and black pepper.

4. **Stuff the Mushrooms:**

   - Once the mushrooms are cooked and slightly cooled, stuff them with the caprese filling mixture.

5. **Serve:**

   - Drizzle with balsamic glaze and garnish with fresh basil leaves.

- Serve the Caprese Stuffed Portobello Mushrooms warm.

Nutritional Information (Per Serving, 1 Mushroom):

- Calories: 160

- Protein: 8g

- Carbohydrates: 6g

- Fiber: 2g

- Sugars: 3g

- Fat: 12g

- Saturated Fat: 5g

- Cholesterol: 20mg

- Sodium: 250mg

- Vitamin C: 10% DV

- Vitamin A: 10% DV

- Iron: 4% DV

Summary:

These Caprese Stuffed Portobello Mushrooms are a protein-rich and flavorful dish that combines portobello mushrooms with a classic caprese salad filling. It's a delightful and elegant option for a healthy lunch or appetizer.

Tips and Tricks:

- Customize with your favorite herbs or add a sprinkle of pine nuts for extra crunch.

- Drizzle with extra balsamic glaze before serving for added flavor.

Ingredient Substitutions:

- Use cherry or grape tomatoes instead of cherry tomato halves.

Mediterranean Tuna Salad

Ingredients:

- 2 cans (5 ounces each) tuna in water, drained
- 1 cucumber, diced
- 1 cup cherry tomatoes, halved
- 1/4 cup red onion, finely chopped
- 1/4 cup Kalamata olives, pitted and sliced
- 1/4 cup feta cheese, crumbled
- 2 tablespoons fresh parsley, chopped
- Juice of 1 lemon
- 2 tablespoons olive oil
- Salt and black pepper, to taste
- Mixed salad greens, for serving

Instructions:

1. **Prepare the Salad:**

   - In a large bowl, combine drained tuna, diced cucumber, halved cherry tomatoes, finely chopped red onion, sliced Kalamata olives, crumbled feta cheese, and chopped fresh parsley.

2. **Make the Dressing:**

   - In a small bowl, whisk together lemon juice and olive oil.

   - Season with salt and black pepper.

3. **Combine and Serve:**

   - Drizzle the dressing over the salad ingredients.

   - Gently toss everything together until well coated.

   - Serve over mixed salad greens.

Nutritional Information (Per Serving):

- Calories: 280

- Protein: 30g

- Carbohydrates: 8g

- Fiber: 2g

- Sugars: 3g

- Fat: 14g

- Saturated Fat: 3g

- Cholesterol: 35mg

- Sodium: 480mg

- Vitamin C: 30% DV

- Vitamin A: 15% DV

- Iron: 10% DV

Summary:

This Mediterranean Tuna Salad is a protein-packed and flavorful dish that combines tuna, cucumber, cherry tomatoes, olives, and feta cheese with a zesty lemon dressing. It's a satisfying and healthy lunch option.

Tips and Tricks:

- Customize with your favorite Mediterranean ingredients like roasted red peppers or artichoke hearts.

- Serve with a side of whole wheat pita bread.

Ingredient Substitutions:

- Use canned salmon or grilled chicken as a substitute for tuna.

Broccoli and Cheddar Stuffed Sweet Potatoes

Ingredients:

- 4 medium sweet potatoes
- 2 cups broccoli florets, steamed and chopped
- 1 cup shredded cheddar cheese
- 1/4 cup Greek yogurt (non-fat or low-fat)
- 2 tablespoons chopped chives
- Salt and black pepper, to taste
- Olive oil, for drizzling

Instructions:

1. **Prepare the Sweet Potatoes:**

   - Preheat your oven to 400°F (200°C).
   - Pierce sweet potatoes with a fork and place them on a baking sheet.
   - Drizzle with a bit of olive oil and sprinkle with salt.

- Bake for about 45-60 minutes, or until the sweet potatoes are tender and can be easily pierced with a fork.

2. **Cut and Stuff the Potatoes:**

   - Slice each sweet potato lengthwise and fluff the flesh with a fork.

   - Top each sweet potato half with steamed and chopped broccoli florets.

3. **Add Cheddar and Yogurt:**

   - Sprinkle shredded cheddar cheese over the broccoli.

   - Dollop Greek yogurt on top.

   - Season with salt and black pepper.

4. **Serve:**

   - Garnish with chopped chives.

   - Serve the Broccoli and Cheddar Stuffed Sweet Potatoes hot.

Nutritional Information (Per Serving, 1 Stuffed Sweet Potato Half):

- Calories: 250

- Protein: 10g

- Carbohydrates: 35g

- Fiber: 6g

- Sugars: 8g

- Fat: 8g

- Saturated Fat: 5g

- Cholesterol: 25mg

- Sodium: 270mg

- Vitamin C: 70% DV

- Vitamin A: 370% DV

- Iron: 10% DV

Summary:

These Broccoli and Cheddar Stuffed Sweet Potatoes are a protein-rich and nutritious option for a healthy lunch or dinner. The sweet potatoes are stuffed with steamed broccoli, cheddar cheese, Greek yogurt, and chives for a delicious combination of flavors.

Tips and Tricks:

- Customize with your favorite toppings like diced tomatoes or bacon bits.

- Drizzle with hot sauce for a spicy kick.

Ingredient Substitutions:

- Use cauliflower florets as a substitute for broccoli.

Teriyaki Salmon and Vegetable Foil Packets

Ingredients:

- 2 salmon fillets
- 2 cups broccoli florets
- 1 red bell pepper, sliced
- 1 yellow bell pepper, sliced
- 1 carrot, thinly sliced
- 1/4 cup teriyaki sauce (low-sodium)
- 2 tablespoons olive oil
- 1 tablespoon sesame seeds
- Salt and black pepper, to taste
- Cooked brown rice, for serving

Instructions:

1. **Preheat the Grill or Oven:**

   - Preheat your grill to medium-high heat or preheat your oven to 400°F (200°C).

2. **Prepare Foil Packets:**

   - Tear off two large pieces of aluminum foil.

   - Place half of the broccoli florets, sliced red bell pepper, sliced yellow bell pepper, and thinly sliced carrot on each piece of foil.

3. **Season and Add Salmon:**

   - Season the salmon fillets with salt and black pepper.

   - Place one salmon fillet on top of the vegetables on each foil piece.

4. **Drizzle and Seal:**

   - In a small bowl, whisk together teriyaki sauce and olive oil.

   - Drizzle the teriyaki mixture over the salmon and vegetables.

   - Seal the foil packets by folding them over and crimping the edges tightly.

5. **Grill or Bake:**

   - If grilling, place the foil packets directly on the grill grates.

- If baking, place them on a baking sheet.

- Grill or bake for about 15-20 minutes, or until the salmon is cooked through and flakes easily.

6. **Serve:**

- Carefully open the foil packets.

- Sprinkle with sesame seeds.

- Serve the Teriyaki Salmon and Vegetable Foil Packets over cooked brown rice.

Nutritional Information (Per Serving):

- Calories: 380

- Protein: 30g

- Carbohydrates: 30g

- Fiber: 6g

- Sugars: 12g

- Fat: 16g

- Saturated Fat: 2.5g

- Cholesterol: 60mg

- Sodium: 550mg

- Vitamin C: 230% DV

- Vitamin A: 180% DV

- Iron: 15% DV

Summary:

These Teriyaki Salmon and Vegetable Foil Packets are a protein-packed and flavorful option for a healthy lunch or dinner. The salmon and colorful vegetables are cooked in a delicious teriyaki sauce and served over brown rice.

Tips and Tricks:

- Customize with your favorite vegetables or add pineapple chunks for sweetness.

- Drizzle with extra teriyaki sauce before serving for added flavor.

Ingredient Substitutions:

- Use chicken breast or tofu as a substitute for salmon.

Spinach and Mushroom Quiche

Ingredients:

- 1 prepared pie crust (store-bought or homemade)
- 1 cup fresh spinach leaves, chopped
- 1 cup mushrooms, sliced
- 1/2 cup shredded Swiss cheese
- 4 large eggs
- 1 cup milk (2% or whole)
- Salt and black pepper, to taste
- Pinch of nutmeg (optional)
- Fresh thyme leaves, for garnish (optional)

Instructions:

1. **Preheat the Oven:**

   - Preheat your oven to 375°F (190°C).

2. **Prepare the Crust:**

   - Place the prepared pie crust in a pie dish and crimp the edges.

3. **Sauté Spinach and Mushrooms:**

   - In a skillet, sauté chopped fresh spinach and sliced mushrooms over medium heat until they are slightly wilted and any excess moisture from the mushrooms has evaporated.

   - Season with salt and black pepper.

4. **Layer Ingredients:**

   - Spread the sautéed spinach and mushrooms evenly over the bottom of the pie crust.

   - Sprinkle shredded Swiss cheese on top.

5. **Make the Quiche Mixture:**

   - In a bowl, whisk together eggs, milk, a pinch of nutmeg (if using), salt, and black pepper.

6. **Pour and Bake:**

   - Pour the egg mixture over the spinach, mushrooms, and cheese in the pie crust.

- Bake in the preheated oven for about 35-40 minutes, or until the quiche is set and the top is golden brown.

7. **Serve:**

- Garnish with fresh thyme leaves if desired.
- Serve the Spinach and Mushroom Quiche warm or at room temperature.

Nutritional Information (Per Serving, 1 Slice):

- Calories: 230
- Protein: 9g
- Carbohydrates: 14g
- Fiber: 1g
- Sugars: 2g
- Fat: 15g
- Saturated Fat: 7g
- Cholesterol: 105mg
- Sodium: 290mg
- Vitamin C: 6% DV

- Vitamin A: 25% DV

- Iron: 6% DV

Summary:

This Spinach and Mushroom Quiche is a protein-rich and savory dish that combines fresh spinach, mushrooms, and Swiss cheese in a flaky pie crust. It's a delightful option for a wholesome lunch or brunch.

Tips and Tricks:

- Customize with your favorite vegetables or add cooked bacon for extra flavor.

- Serve with a side salad for a complete meal.

Ingredient Substitutions:

- Use cheddar, mozzarella, or feta cheese as a substitute for Swiss cheese.

Shrimp and Avocado Salad

Ingredients:

- 1 pound large shrimp, peeled and deveined
- 2 avocados, diced
- 1 cup cherry tomatoes, halved
- 1/4 cup red onion, finely chopped
- 1/4 cup fresh cilantro, chopped
- Juice of 2 limes
- 2 tablespoons olive oil
- Salt and black pepper, to taste
- Mixed salad greens, for serving

Instructions:

1. **Cook the Shrimp:**

   - In a skillet, heat a bit of olive oil over medium-high heat.
   - Add shrimp and cook for about 2-3 minutes per side, or until they are pink and opaque.

- Season with salt and black pepper.

2. **Prepare the Salad:**

   - In a large bowl, combine diced avocados, halved cherry tomatoes, finely chopped red onion, and chopped fresh cilantro.

3. **Make the Dressing:**

   - In a small bowl, whisk together lime juice and olive oil.

   - Season with salt and black pepper.

4. **Combine and Serve:**

   - Add cooked shrimp to the salad ingredients.

   - Drizzle the dressing over the salad.

   - Gently toss everything together until well coated.

   - Serve the Shrimp and Avocado Salad over mixed salad greens.

Nutritional Information (Per Serving):

- Calories: 330

- Protein: 25g

- Carbohydrates: 14g

- Fiber: 7g

- Sugars: 2g

- Fat: 21g

- Saturated Fat: 3g

- Cholesterol: 180mg

- Sodium: 380mg

- Vitamin C: 40% DV

- Vitamin A: 20% DV

- Iron: 15% DV

Summary:

This Shrimp and Avocado Salad is a protein-packed and refreshing dish that combines succulent shrimp, diced avocado, cherry tomatoes, and cilantro with a zesty lime dressing. It's a light and healthy lunch option.

Tips and Tricks:

- Customize with your favorite herbs or add a pinch of chili flakes for extra spice.

- Drizzle with extra lime juice before serving for added zest.

Ingredient Substitutions:

- Use cooked chicken breast or tofu as a substitute for shrimp.

Black Bean and Quinoa Stuffed Bell Peppers

Ingredients:

- 4 bell peppers, any color
- 1 cup cooked quinoa
- 1 (15-ounce) can black beans, drained and rinsed
- 1 cup corn kernels (fresh, frozen, or canned)
- 1 cup diced tomatoes (canned or fresh)
- 1/2 cup shredded cheddar cheese
- 1 teaspoon chili powder
- 1/2 teaspoon ground cumin
- Salt and black pepper, to taste
- Fresh cilantro, for garnish (optional)

Instructions:

1. **Preheat the Oven:**

   - Preheat your oven to 375°F (190°C).

2. **Prepare the Peppers:**

- Cut the tops off the bell peppers and remove the seeds and membranes from the inside.

3. **Prepare the Filling:**

   - In a large bowl, combine cooked quinoa, drained black beans, corn kernels, diced tomatoes, shredded cheddar cheese, chili powder, ground cumin, salt, and black pepper.

4. **Stuff the Peppers:**

   - Fill each bell pepper with the quinoa and black bean mixture.

5. **Bake:**

   - Place the stuffed peppers in a baking dish and cover with aluminum foil.

   - Bake in the preheated oven for about 25-30 minutes, or until the peppers are tender.

6. **Serve:**

   - Garnish with fresh cilantro if desired.

- Serve the Black Bean and Quinoa Stuffed Bell Peppers hot.

Nutritional Information (Per Serving, 1 Stuffed Bell Pepper):

- Calories: 280

- Protein: 11g

- Carbohydrates: 50g

- Fiber: 9g

- Sugars: 6g

- Fat: 6g

- Saturated Fat: 3g

- Cholesterol: 15mg

- Sodium: 390mg

- Vitamin C: 190% DV

- Vitamin A: 110% DV

- Iron: 10% DV

Summary:

These Black Bean and Quinoa Stuffed Bell Peppers are a protein-rich and wholesome dish that combines bell peppers filled with a flavorful mixture of quinoa, black beans, corn, and cheese. It's a satisfying and nutritious lunch or dinner.

Tips and Tricks:

- Customize with your favorite vegetables or add a dollop of Greek yogurt on top.

- Experiment with different cheese varieties for added flavor.

Ingredient Substitutions:

- Use brown rice or couscous as a substitute for quinoa.

Thai Peanut Tofu and Noodle Bowl

Ingredients:

- 8 ounces rice noodles

- 1 block extra-firm tofu, cubed

- 2 cups broccoli florets

- 1 red bell pepper, thinly sliced

- 1 carrot, julienned

- 1/4 cup creamy peanut butter

- 2 tablespoons soy sauce (low-sodium)

- 2 tablespoons rice vinegar

- 1 tablespoon honey

- 1 teaspoon sesame oil

- 1 clove garlic, minced

- 1/2 teaspoon grated fresh ginger

- Crushed peanuts and chopped cilantro, for garnish (optional)

Instructions:

1. **Cook the Noodles:**

   - Cook rice noodles according to package instructions.

   - Drain and set aside.

2. **Prepare the Tofu:**

   - Press tofu to remove excess water, then cut it into cubes.

   - Heat a bit of olive oil in a skillet over medium heat.

   - Add tofu cubes and cook until they are golden brown on all sides.

   - Remove tofu from the skillet and set aside.

3. **Blanch the Broccoli:**

   - In the same skillet, blanch broccoli florets by cooking them in boiling water for about 2 minutes.

   - Drain and set aside.

4. **Make the Peanut Sauce:**

- In a bowl, whisk together creamy peanut butter, soy sauce, rice vinegar, honey, sesame oil, minced garlic, and grated fresh ginger.

- Adjust the sauce to your taste by adding more soy sauce or honey if needed.

5. **Combine Ingredients:**

   - In a large bowl, combine cooked rice noodles, cooked tofu, blanched broccoli, sliced red bell pepper, and julienned carrot.

6. **Toss with Peanut Sauce:**

   - Pour the peanut sauce over the noodle and vegetable mixture.

   - Gently toss everything together until well coated.

7. **Serve:**

   - Garnish with crushed peanuts and chopped cilantro if desired.

   - Serve the Thai Peanut Tofu and Noodle Bowl warm.

Nutritional Information (Per Serving):

- Calories: 450

- Protein: 18g

- Carbohydrates: 60g

- Fiber: 6g

- Sugars: 9g

- Fat: 17g

- Saturated Fat: 3g

- Cholesterol: 0mg

- Sodium: 480mg

- Vitamin C: 80% DV

- Vitamin A: 90% DV

- Iron: 15% DV

Summary:

This Thai Peanut Tofu and Noodle Bowl is a protein-rich and flavorful dish that combines rice noodles, crispy tofu, fresh vegetables, and a creamy peanut sauce. It's a delicious and satisfying option for a hearty lunch or dinner.

Tips and Tricks:

- Customize with your favorite vegetables or add a squeeze of lime juice for extra zest.

- For added protein, use edamame or cooked chicken breast instead of tofu.

Ingredient Substitutions:

- Use almond butter or cashew butter as a substitute for peanut butter.

Greek Chicken Souvlaki Skewers

Ingredients:

- 1 pound boneless, skinless chicken breasts, cut into cubes
- 1 red onion, cut into chunks
- 1 red bell pepper, cut into chunks
- 1 yellow bell pepper, cut into chunks
- 1/4 cup plain Greek yogurt
- 2 tablespoons olive oil
- 2 cloves garlic, minced
- 1 teaspoon dried oregano
- Juice of 1 lemon
- Salt and black pepper, to taste
- Wooden skewers, soaked in water

Instructions:

1. **Prepare the Marinade:**

- In a bowl, whisk together plain Greek yogurt, olive oil, minced garlic, dried oregano, lemon juice, salt, and black pepper.

2. **Marinate the Chicken:**

   - Place the chicken cubes in a resealable plastic bag or shallow dish.

   - Pour the marinade over the chicken and toss to coat.

   - Seal the bag or cover the dish and refrigerate for at least 30 minutes, or ideally, for a few hours.

3. **Assemble the Skewers:**

   - Preheat your grill or grill pan to medium-high heat.

   - Thread marinated chicken, red onion chunks, and bell pepper chunks onto wooden skewers, alternating between the ingredients.

4. **Grill:**

   - Grill the skewers for about 10-15 minutes, turning occasionally, until the chicken is cooked through and the vegetables are tender.

5. **Serve:**

   - Serve the Greek Chicken Souvlaki Skewers hot, accompanied by pita bread and Tzatziki sauce if desired.

Nutritional Information (Per Serving):

- Calories: 280

- Protein: 30g

- Carbohydrates: 8g

- Fiber: 2g

- Sugars: 4g

- Fat: 14g

- Saturated Fat: 2g

- Cholesterol: 75mg

- Sodium: 320mg

- Vitamin C: 120% DV

- Vitamin A: 20% DV

- Iron: 8% DV

Summary:

These Greek Chicken Souvlaki Skewers are a protein-packed and flavorful dish that features marinated chicken, red onion, and bell peppers grilled to perfection. They are a delightful and healthy option for a satisfying lunch or dinner.

Tips and Tricks:

- Use metal skewers to avoid soaking wooden ones.

- Serve with a side of rice or a Greek salad for a complete meal.

Ingredient Substitutions:

- Use boneless, skinless chicken thighs instead of chicken breasts.

Spaghetti Squash with Pesto and Cherry Tomatoes

Ingredients:

- 1 spaghetti squash

- 1 cup cherry tomatoes, halved

- 1/4 cup pesto sauce (homemade or store-bought)

- 2 tablespoons grated Parmesan cheese

- Fresh basil leaves, for garnish (optional)

- Olive oil, for drizzling

- Salt and black pepper, to taste

Instructions:

1. **Preheat the Oven:**

   - Preheat your oven to 375°F (190°C).

2. **Prepare the Squash:**

   - Carefully cut the spaghetti squash in half lengthwise.

- Scoop out the seeds and pulp.

- Drizzle the cut sides of the squash with olive oil and season with salt and black pepper.

3. **Roast the Squash:**

- Place the squash halves, cut side down, on a baking sheet.

- Roast in the preheated oven for about 30-40 minutes, or until the squash flesh is tender and easily shreds with a fork.

- Let it cool slightly.

4. **Scrape and Serve:**

- Use a fork to scrape the spaghetti-like strands of squash from the shells.

- Place the squash "noodles" in a large bowl.

5. **Add Tomatoes and Pesto:**

- Add halved cherry tomatoes and pesto sauce to the bowl with the squash.

- Toss everything together until well combined.

6. **Serve:**

   - Garnish with grated Parmesan cheese and fresh basil leaves if desired.

   - Serve the Spaghetti Squash with Pesto and Cherry Tomatoes warm.

Nutritional Information (Per Serving):

- Calories: 250

- Protein: 4g

- Carbohydrates: 18g

- Fiber: 4g

- Sugars: 7g

- Fat: 19g

- Saturated Fat: 3.5g

- Cholesterol: 5mg

- Sodium: 370mg

- Vitamin C: 30% DV

- Vitamin A: 25% DV

- Iron: 10% DV

Summary:

This Spaghetti Squash with Pesto and Cherry Tomatoes is a healthy and flavorful dish that features roasted spaghetti squash tossed with pesto and fresh cherry tomatoes. It's a light and satisfying option for a nutritious lunch or dinner.

Tips and Tricks:

- Customize with your favorite vegetables or add grilled chicken for extra protein.

- Use homemade pesto for the freshest flavor.

Ingredient Substitutions:

- Use zucchini noodles (zoodles) as a substitute for spaghetti squash.

Quinoa and Black Bean Stuffed Peppers

Ingredients:

- 4 large bell peppers, any color

- 1 cup cooked quinoa

- 1 (15-ounce) can black beans, drained and rinsed

- 1 cup corn kernels (fresh, frozen, or canned)

- 1 cup diced tomatoes (canned or fresh)

- 1/2 cup shredded cheddar cheese

- 1 teaspoon chili powder

- 1/2 teaspoon ground cumin

- Salt and black pepper, to taste

- Fresh cilantro, for garnish (optional)

Instructions:

1. **Preheat the Oven:**

   - Preheat your oven to 375°F (190°C).

2. **Prepare the Peppers:**

- Cut the tops off the bell peppers and remove the seeds and membranes from the inside.

3. **Prepare the Filling:**

   - In a large bowl, combine cooked quinoa, drained black beans, corn kernels, diced tomatoes, shredded cheddar cheese, chili powder, ground cumin, salt, and black pepper.

4. **Stuff the Peppers:**

   - Fill each bell pepper with the quinoa and black bean mixture.

5. **Bake:**

   - Place the stuffed peppers in a baking dish and cover with aluminum foil.

   - Bake in the preheated oven for about 25-30 minutes, or until the peppers are tender.

6. **Serve:**

   - Garnish with fresh cilantro if desired.

- Serve the Quinoa and Black Bean Stuffed Peppers hot.

Nutritional Information (Per Serving, 1 Stuffed Bell Pepper):

- Calories: 280

- Protein: 11g

- Carbohydrates: 50g

- Fiber: 9g

- Sugars: 6g

- Fat: 6g

- Saturated Fat: 3g

- Cholesterol: 15mg

- Sodium: 390mg

- Vitamin C: 190% DV

- Vitamin A: 110% DV

- Iron: 10% DV

Summary:

These Quinoa and Black Bean Stuffed Peppers are a protein-rich and wholesome dish that combines bell peppers filled with a flavorful mixture of quinoa, black beans, corn, and cheese. It's a satisfying and nutritious lunch or dinner.

Tips and Tricks:

- Customize with your favorite vegetables or add a dollop of Greek yogurt on top.

- Experiment with different cheese varieties for added flavor.

Ingredient Substitutions:

- Use brown rice or couscous as a substitute for quinoa.

Thai Peanut Tofu and Noodle Bowl

Ingredients:

- 8 ounces rice noodles

- 1 block extra-firm tofu, cubed

- 2 cups broccoli florets

- 1 red bell pepper, thinly sliced

- 1 carrot, julienned

- 1/4 cup creamy peanut butter

- 2 tablespoons soy sauce (low-sodium)

- 2 tablespoons rice vinegar

- 1 tablespoon honey

- 1 teaspoon sesame oil

- 1 clove garlic, minced

- 1/2 teaspoon grated fresh ginger

- Crushed peanuts and chopped cilantro, for garnish (optional)

Instructions:

1. **Cook the Noodles:**

   - Cook rice noodles according to package instructions.

   - Drain and set aside.

2. **Prepare the Tofu:**

   - Press tofu to remove excess water, then cut it into cubes.

   - Heat a bit of olive oil in a skillet over medium heat.

   - Add tofu cubes and cook until they are golden brown on all sides.

   - Remove tofu from the skillet and set aside.

3. **Blanch the Broccoli:**

   - In the same skillet, blanch broccoli florets by cooking them in boiling water for about 2 minutes.

   - Drain and set aside.

4. **Make the Peanut Sauce:**

- In a bowl, whisk together creamy peanut butter, soy sauce, rice vinegar, honey, sesame oil, minced garlic, and grated fresh ginger.

- Adjust the sauce to your taste by adding more soy sauce or honey if needed.

5. **Combine Ingredients:**

- In a large bowl, combine cooked rice noodles, cooked tofu, blanched broccoli, sliced red bell pepper, and julienned carrot.

6. **Toss with Peanut Sauce:**

- Pour the peanut sauce over the noodle and vegetable mixture.

- Gently toss everything together until well coated.

7. **Serve:**

- Garnish with crushed peanuts and chopped cilantro if desired.

- Serve the Thai Peanut Tofu and Noodle Bowl warm.

Nutritional Information (Per Serving):

- Calories: 450
- Protein: 18g
- Carbohydrates: 60g
- Fiber: 6g
- Sugars: 9g
- Fat: 17g
- Saturated Fat: 3g
- Cholesterol: 0mg
- Sodium: 480mg
- Vitamin C: 80% DV
- Vitamin A: 90% DV
- Iron: 15% DV

Summary:

This Thai Peanut Tofu and Noodle Bowl is a protein-packed and flavorful dish that combines rice noodles, crispy tofu, fresh vegetables, and a creamy peanut sauce. It's a delicious and satisfying option for a hearty lunch or dinner.

Tips and Tricks:

- Customize with your favorite vegetables or add a squeeze of lime juice for extra zest.

- For added protein, use edamame or cooked chicken breast instead of tofu.

Ingredient Substitutions:

- Use almond butter or cashew butter as a substitute for peanut butter.

Mediterranean Quinoa Salad

Ingredients:

- 1 cup cooked quinoa

- 1 cucumber, diced

- 1 cup cherry tomatoes, halved

- 1/2 cup Kalamata olives, pitted and sliced

- 1/2 cup crumbled feta cheese

- 1/4 cup red onion, finely chopped

- 2 tablespoons fresh parsley, chopped

- Juice of 1 lemon

- 2 tablespoons olive oil

- Salt and black pepper, to taste

Instructions:

1. **Prepare the Salad:**

   - In a large bowl, combine cooked quinoa, diced cucumber, halved cherry tomatoes, sliced Kalamata olives, crumbled feta cheese, finely chopped red onion, and chopped fresh parsley.

2. **Make the Dressing:**

   - In a small bowl, whisk together lemon juice and olive oil.

   - Season with salt and black pepper.

3. **Combine and Serve:**

   - Drizzle the dressing over the salad ingredients.

   - Gently toss everything together until well coated.

   - Serve the Mediterranean Quinoa Salad chilled.

Nutritional Information (Per Serving):

- Calories: 320

- Protein: 8g

- Carbohydrates: 30g

- Fiber: 5g

- Sugars: 3g

- Fat: 20g

- Saturated Fat: 5g

- Cholesterol: 20mg

- Sodium: 520mg

- Vitamin C: 30% DV

- Vitamin A: 10% DV

- Iron: 15% DV

Summary:

This Mediterranean Quinoa Salad is a protein-rich and refreshing dish that combines cooked quinoa with cucumber, cherry tomatoes, Kalamata olives, feta cheese, and a zesty lemon dressing. It's a perfect choice for a light and healthy lunch or side dish.

Tips and Tricks:

- Customize with your favorite Mediterranean ingredients like roasted red peppers or artichoke hearts.

- Add grilled chicken or chickpeas for extra protein.

Ingredient Substitutions:

- Use couscous or bulgur as a substitute for quinoa.

Lemon Garlic Shrimp and Asparagus

Ingredients:

- 1 pound large shrimp, peeled and deveined
- 1 bunch asparagus, trimmed
- 3 cloves garlic, minced
- Juice of 2 lemons
- 2 tablespoons olive oil
- 1 teaspoon dried oregano
- Salt and black pepper, to taste
- Fresh parsley, for garnish (optional)

Instructions:

1. **Marinate the Shrimp:**

   - In a bowl, combine peeled and deveined shrimp with minced garlic, lemon juice, olive oil, dried oregano, salt, and black pepper.
   - Toss to coat and let it marinate for about 10-15 minutes.

2. **Sauté Asparagus:**

- Heat a large skillet over medium-high heat.

- Add trimmed asparagus to the skillet and sauté for about 5-7 minutes, or until they are tender-crisp and lightly charred.

- Remove asparagus from the skillet and set aside.

3. **Cook the Shrimp:**

- In the same skillet, add marinated shrimp in a single layer.

- Cook for about 2-3 minutes per side, or until they are pink and opaque.

4. **Serve:**

- Serve the Lemon Garlic Shrimp and Asparagus hot.

- Garnish with fresh parsley if desired.

Nutritional Information (Per Serving):

- Calories: 220

- Protein: 25g

- Carbohydrates: 7g

- Fiber: 3g

- Sugars: 2g

- Fat: 10g

- Saturated Fat: 1.5g

- Cholesterol: 180mg

- Sodium: 290mg

- Vitamin C: 45% DV

- Vitamin A: 20% DV

- Iron: 15% DV

Summary:

This Lemon Garlic Shrimp and Asparagus dish is a protein-packed and vibrant option for a healthy lunch or dinner. It features marinated shrimp cooked to perfection with tender-crisp asparagus in a zesty lemon and garlic sauce.

Tips and Tricks:

- Customize with your favorite herbs or add a pinch of red pepper flakes for a kick of spice.

- Serve over cooked brown rice or quinoa for a heartier meal.

Ingredient Substitutions:

- Use green beans or broccoli as a substitute for asparagus.

Chickpea and Vegetable Stir-Fry

Ingredients:

- 2 cups cooked chickpeas (canned or cooked from dried)
- 2 cups mixed vegetables (bell peppers, broccoli, snap peas, carrots, etc.), chopped
- 2 cloves garlic, minced
- 2 tablespoons low-sodium soy sauce
- 1 tablespoon honey
- 1 teaspoon sesame oil
- 1/2 teaspoon ground ginger
- 1/4 teaspoon red pepper flakes (adjust to taste)
- Olive oil, for cooking
- Cooked brown rice or quinoa, for serving

Instructions:

1. **Prepare the Sauce:**

- In a small bowl, whisk together low-sodium soy sauce, honey, sesame oil, minced garlic, ground ginger, and red pepper flakes.

2. **Sauté Vegetables:**

   - Heat a bit of olive oil in a large skillet or wok over medium-high heat.

   - Add chopped mixed vegetables to the skillet and stir-fry for about 3-5 minutes, or until they are tender-crisp.

   - Remove vegetables from the skillet and set aside.

3. **Stir-Fry Chickpeas:**

   - In the same skillet, add cooked chickpeas.

   - Stir-fry for about 2-3 minutes until they are heated through and slightly crispy.

4. **Combine and Serve:**

   - Return the sautéed vegetables to the skillet with the chickpeas.

   - Pour the sauce over the chickpeas and vegetables.

- Stir-fry everything together for another 2-3 minutes, ensuring the sauce coats the mixture evenly.

5. **Serve:**

- Serve the Chickpea and Vegetable Stir-Fry hot, over cooked brown rice or quinoa.

Nutritional Information (Per Serving, without rice or quinoa):

- Calories: 280

- Protein: 10g

- Carbohydrates: 45g

- Fiber: 9g

- Sugars: 11g

- Fat: 7g

- Saturated Fat: 1g

- Cholesterol: 0mg

- Sodium: 370mg

- Vitamin C: 60% DV

- Vitamin A: 80% DV

- Iron: 15% DV

Summary:

This Chickpea and Vegetable Stir-Fry is a protein-rich and colorful dish that combines sautéed mixed vegetables and crispy chickpeas in a flavorful sauce. It's a quick and healthy option for a satisfying lunch or dinner.

Tips and Tricks:

- Customize with your favorite vegetables or add tofu for extra protein.

- Adjust the level of spiciness by adding more or fewer red pepper flakes.

Ingredient Substitutions:

- Use maple syrup or agave nectar as a substitute for honey.

Tuna and White Bean Salad

Ingredients:

- 2 cans (5 ounces each) canned tuna in water, drained
- 1 can (15 ounces) white beans (cannellini or Great Northern), drained and rinsed
- 1/2 cup red onion, finely chopped
- 1/2 cup celery, finely chopped
- 1/4 cup fresh parsley, chopped
- Juice of 1 lemon
- 2 tablespoons olive oil
- Salt and black pepper, to taste
- Mixed salad greens, for serving

Instructions:

1. **Prepare the Salad:**

   - In a large bowl, combine drained canned tuna, white beans, finely chopped red onion, finely chopped celery, and chopped fresh parsley.

2. **Make the Dressing:**

   - In a small bowl, whisk together lemon juice, olive oil, salt, and black pepper.

3. **Combine and Serve:**

   - Drizzle the dressing over the tuna and white bean mixture.

   - Gently toss everything together until well coated.

4. **Serve:**

   - Serve the Tuna and White Bean Salad over mixed salad greens.

Nutritional Information (Per Serving, salad only, without greens):

- Calories: 320

- Protein: 26g

- Carbohydrates: 20g

- Fiber: 6g

- Sugars: 2g

- Fat: 15g

- Saturated Fat: 2g

- Cholesterol: 25mg

- Sodium: 480mg

- Vitamin C: 15% DV

- Vitamin A: 4% DV

- Iron: 20% DV

Summary:

This Tuna and White Bean Salad is a protein-packed and satisfying dish that combines canned tuna, white beans, red onion, celery, and fresh parsley in a zesty lemon dressing. It's a simple and nutritious option for a quick lunch or dinner.

Tips and Tricks:

- Customize with your favorite herbs or add chopped pickles for extra flavor.

- Serve with whole-grain crackers or bread for a complete meal.

Ingredient Substitutions:

- Use canned salmon or cooked chicken as a substitute for tuna.

Mexican Quinoa Bowl

Ingredients:

- 1 cup cooked quinoa
- 1 cup cooked black beans (canned or cooked from dried)
- 1 cup corn kernels (fresh, frozen, or canned)
- 1 cup cherry tomatoes, halved
- 1/2 cup red bell pepper, diced
- 1/2 cup avocado, diced
- 1/4 cup red onion, finely chopped
- 2 tablespoons fresh cilantro, chopped
- Juice of 2 limes
- 2 tablespoons olive oil
- 1 teaspoon chili powder
- 1/2 teaspoon ground cumin
- Salt and black pepper, to taste

Instructions:

1. **Prepare the Bowl:**

   - In a large bowl, combine cooked quinoa, cooked black beans, corn kernels, halved cherry tomatoes, diced red bell pepper, diced avocado, finely chopped red onion, and chopped fresh cilantro.

2. **Make the Dressing:**

   - In a small bowl, whisk together lime juice, olive oil, chili powder, ground cumin, salt, and black pepper.

3. **Combine and Serve:**

   - Drizzle the dressing over the quinoa and vegetable mixture.

   - Gently toss everything together until well coated.

4. **Serve:**

   - Serve the Mexican Quinoa Bowl as a hearty and nutritious lunch or dinner.

Nutritional Information (Per Serving):

- Calories: 350

- Protein: 10g

- Carbohydrates: 48g

- Fiber: 11g

- Sugars: 5g

- Fat: 15g

- Saturated Fat: 2g

- Cholesterol: 0mg

- Sodium: 260mg

- Vitamin C: 40% DV

- Vitamin A: 15% DV

- Iron: 20% DV

Summary:

This Mexican Quinoa Bowl is a protein-rich and flavorful dish that combines quinoa, black beans, corn, cherry tomatoes, avocado, and red pepper in a zesty lime dressing. It's a vibrant and satisfying option for a wholesome lunch or dinner.

Tips and Tricks:

- Customize with your favorite toppings like shredded cheese or jalapeños for added heat.

- Add cooked ground turkey or beef for extra protein.

Ingredient Substitutions:

- Use brown rice or couscous as a substitute for quinoa.

Lemon Herb Grilled Salmon

Ingredients:

- 4 salmon fillets (6 ounces each)
- Juice of 2 lemons
- 2 tablespoons olive oil
- 2 cloves garlic, minced
- 2 tablespoons fresh herbs (such as dill, parsley, or basil), chopped
- Salt and black pepper, to taste
- Lemon wedges, for garnish (optional)

Instructions:

1. **Prepare the Marinade:**

   - In a bowl, whisk together lemon juice, olive oil, minced garlic, chopped fresh herbs, salt, and black pepper.

2. **Marinate the Salmon:**

   - Place salmon fillets in a resealable plastic bag or shallow dish.

- Pour the marinade over the salmon and ensure it is evenly coated.
- Seal the bag or cover the dish and refrigerate for at least 30 minutes.

3. **Grill:**

- Preheat your grill to medium-high heat.
- Remove the salmon from the marinade and discard the marinade.
- Grill the salmon fillets for about 3-4 minutes per side, or until they are cooked through and have grill marks.

4. **Serve:**

- Serve the Lemon Herb Grilled Salmon hot.
- Garnish with lemon wedges if desired.

Nutritional Information (Per Serving):

- Calories: 350
- Protein: 34g
- Carbohydrates: 3g
- Fiber: 1g

- Sugars: 0g

- Fat: 23g

- Saturated Fat: 4g

- Cholesterol: 95mg

- Sodium: 110mg

- Vitamin C: 35% DV

- Vitamin A: 10% DV

- Iron: 10% DV

Summary:

This Lemon Herb Grilled Salmon is a protein-packed and flavorful dish that features salmon fillets marinated in a zesty lemon and herb mixture, then grilled to perfection. It's a delicious and nutritious option for a satisfying lunch or dinner.

Tips and Tricks:

- Customize with your favorite fresh herbs or add a sprinkle of lemon zest for extra brightness.

- Serve with a side of steamed vegetables or a green salad for a complete meal.

Ingredient Substitutions:

- Use trout or mahi-mahi as a substitute for salmon.

Thank you

Printed in Great Britain
by Amazon

44889304R00119